SILENT INVADER

SILENT INVADER

A Glider Pilot's Story of the Invasion
of Europe in World War II

ALEXANDER MORRISON

Airlife
CLASSIC

This book is a true record of the incidents described although, with a memory gap of 53 years, detail has had to be introduced to support them. Similarly, certain names and ranks have had to be contrived.

First published in the UK in 1999
by **Airlife Publishing Ltd**

This edition published 2002

British Library Cataloguing-in-Publication Data
   A catalogue record for this book
   is available from the British Library

ISBN 1 84037 368 7

Printed in England by Livesey Ltd., Shrewsbury (01743) 235651

Distributed in North America by
STACKPOLE BOOKS
5067 Ritter Road, Mechanicsburg, PA 17055
www.stackpolebooks.com

For a complete list of all Airlife titles please contact:
Airlife Publishing Ltd
101 Longden Road, Shrewsbury, SY3 9EB, England
E-mail: sales@airlifebooks.com
Website: www.airlifebooks.com

CONTENTS

To my wife and to the widows and orphans of the glider
pilots and the RAF crews who towed them,
who died in battle.

PROLOGUE

I suppose it all started on the morning after my twenty-second birthday. I felt absolutely terrible. Indeed, it was only after the fifth black coffee sympathetically administered by my faithful batman, Day, that I was able to sit on the edge of my camp-bed to contemplate, head in hands, the dreadful prospect of facing another day.

'We certainly had a pip of a party in the Mess last night, didn't we sir?' came the unnecessary comment. 'Were we able to climb Everest? The armchairs were five high.' Day, bless him, aspired to become the perfect butler by using the Royal 'we' and by the tone of his voice it sounded as if he was suffering as badly as I was.

'Yes sir, I thought that we might be a little off colour this morning because it is not everyone who is made a Captain on his birthday! However, we do have a problem. The Colonel sent round a message to say that he wants to see you at 10 o'clock sharp.'

'You're pulling my leg, Day. Not this morning please,' I pleaded.

'No sir, it's dinkum.'

'I'll never make it – never! I don't think that I can even stand, let alone salute – the altitude will send me dizzy. I feel like death warmed up!'

'Don't worry sir, I have pressed our best battledress which now proudly displays an extra pip on each side and if I might suggest it, I think that a cold shower will do us a lot of good. Let me assist you down the passage.'

What a gem he was for, with his gentle help, dry toast, aspirins and more coffee, I was finally ready and I must confess that the brisk march from my billet to Battalion Headquarters did much to improve my outlook on life.

Approaching the Adjutant's office door, I knocked quietly and was greeted heartily. 'Hello there John – no I should apologise – hello Captain! I have just sent you a message, didn't you get it? The Colonel has been asked for a Status Report by Brigade and has had to put off your appointment until noon. Sorry old chap, but this must take priority, so would you mind kicking your heels for a couple of hours?'

'Would I mind,' I thought. 'It would be a blessing!'

'Of course sir', I replied, 'but do you know what the Colonel wants to see me about?'

'Yes I do, but I think that he should tell you himself as it seems an exciting challenge. See you at noon then.'

Greatly relieved, I made my way down to Z Company and used the time available, physically and mentally, preparing myself for the interview. At 11.50 a.m. I presented myself once more.

'Ah here you are, the Colonel is expecting you. Go right in and good luck.'

'Why good luck?' I pondered as I knocked on the CO's door.

'Come in, John and sit down. I am sorry I had to postpone our discussion. Firstly, congratulations once more on your Captaincy. It was well earned and the new job that I am about to give you, with its responsibility, will more than justify my decision. I want you to head up a Tank Hunting Unit. It is a new military concept, presumably established in anticipation of a possible German invasion and its task will be to locate enemy tanks in *laager*, attack and put them out of action. It will require tough, fit and brave men and this evening I will hold a meeting of the Company Commanders and will instruct them each to transfer seven of their most suitable chaps to you.

'I understand that you are to be equipped with bicycles which will give you mobility and enable you to operate silently behind the enemy lines. It will take a little while to get this unit established and so I have arranged for you to attend a Tank School to study how they operate and to think out ways and means of harrassing them in action.

'However, before you leave, find premises for your men and choose the best Sergeant for the job. It's a special project John and you are out on your own, so please report regularly on your progress and don't hesitate to ask for help.'

'Thank you sir, I appreciate your confidence.' I saluted and left . . . now completely sober! 'Hells bells, what a job,' I thought, 'hunting Tiger Tanks on bicycles. Oh well, it should be exciting and will provide plenty of scope for cunning tactics.'

My first task was to select a Sergeant and Philips in my Company was just the man. He was a great character, a strict disciplinarian, hard as nails and yet thoughtful and considerate about the welfare of his men. He would have the tremendous task of welding together a complete bunch of strangers to produce what was to be the finest unit in the Battalion. I was thrilled when he jumped at the job and, having made peace with my Company Commander for pinching him, we set forth to find the District Officer and to explain to him our requirements regarding accommodation. Fortunately, he offered us an excellent hall with a kitchen, together with ample ablutions and toilets. This was ideal for us in that the men would live together as a community with plenty of room for lectures and weapon drill.

I then handed over to Sgt Philips and left for the Tank School. During my short stay I learned a good deal about their tactics and returned full of ideas to find that Philips had completely organised the men who seemed happily settled in the quarters which looked spick and span.

Thus was born the Tank Hunting Unit which was to become my pride and joy during my early life as a soldier. Taking stock of the project, I recognised that, whilst the basic attributes of discipline and group loyalty were important, if the men were to survive in action, they would have to be superbly fit and self confident. Accordingly, after the initial training as cyclists, I concentrated on tough and exacting 'battle schemes' and we would set out to all parts of the Pembrokeshire Peninsula for days on end, sleeping rough in the open and living off hard rations. Fortunately it was summer and a dawn plunge into the waves in some little cove would set us up for the day.

At this early stage, I could only assume that we would be supplied with anti-tank and anti-personnel mines and fancy devices such as the 'Sticky Grenade'. This 'Heath Robinson' gadget looked like a small football with a handle. When the pin was pulled, it released a metal surround to reveal a glass bowl covered with a thick gluey compound. The procedure was to creep up to the tank and smash the grenade onto its track where it would explode, but the problem was to keep it away from your own clothing for once it made contact, it stuck fast.

To carry our 'goodies' when they became available would obviously slow us down and so for training, we made up dummy loads strapped on either side of the rear wheel. The freedom of planning our days and the pleasure of organising exacting yet interesting exercises was a happy challenge for me and the men themselves tackled each tiring day with a proud sense of achievement.

Imagine then my personal disappointment when I was called to see the Colonel and given the news that I was to take over Z Company whilst the Commander attended a Staff Course. Admittedly, I suppose it was the route to greater things, but I was to miss the comradeship and independence and was about to return, once more, to stereotype soldiering. This feeling became more acute when the Battalion was transferred to defend a strip of coast in Sussex, and our days were spent building Section strong-points in houses facing the sea, erecting lengths of steel scaffolding which were planted at low tide and stringing miles of barbed-wire in anticipation of the German attack.

I suppose the final straw to my personal frustration was when half my company was taken away and sent out as reinforcements to the Royal Fusilier Battalion fighting in North Africa. Even the Tank Hunting Unit was disbanded! All the training and the happy anticipation of commanding a good fighting unit in battle had been lost and despite my loyalty to the 12th Royal Fusiliers, I decided it was time to make a change. Accordingly, when volunteers were invited for the newly formed Glider Pilot Regiment, I submitted my application in the fervent hope that I would take an active part in the ultimate victory.

I was not disappointed.

ONE

GLIDER PILOT REGIMENT

Interview

For a couple of weeks there was a deathly silence and I assumed that, for some reason, my application had been rejected. Neither had anything dramatic happened in what remained of Z Company and so I decided to take the plunge and proposed to a most wonderful girl. It so happened that her house looked onto the beach and, right from the start, my frequent visits to the proposed strong point in the summer house had had an ulterior motive. Thank goodness she accepted, and we started to make plans to be married in September 1942 because, in war, time is precious.

Indeed, the decision was truly fortuitous for two weeks later I received a summons to attend an interview in Oxford. The selecting officer was Major Billy Griffiths who was then Second-in-Command of No 2 Wing. Pre-war, he had been the English test wicket-keeper and I was able to refresh his memory on a local charity match where I had attempted to bowl quickies for two completely uncontrolled overs at which stage, he had wisely suggested that I needed a rest. He told me that the response calling for volunteers far exceeded both the establishment and the flying training facilities, and that he would only be taking one in seven applicants. Fortunately, subject to a satisfactory medical, I was 'in' and joyfully returned to my company to await further instructions.

Tilshead Camp – Glider Pilot Headquarters

Within a couple of weeks, I received a notification confirming my transfer which was made out to me as a Lieutenant. This was expected because I had been warned that joining officers would be required to drop rank until they had completed their flying training and were posted to an operational squadron. This document instructed me to report to the Rail Transport Officer at Salisbury station by 1500 hrs on 1 June 1942 for conveyance to the Tilshead Camp.

On that day, the total 'volunteers' numbered 5 Officers and 45 other ranks and we really looked a mixed bunch, having been picked from a wide variety of units in the British Army with each sporting different Regimental uniforms and headgear. Although strangers, the excitement of our new adventure brought couples together and I chummed up with Norman Hardie, who turned out to be a wonderful friend, and we stayed together throughout our training. He joined me in the front of our truck and, in due course, we set off.

As we were to be assigned to a brand new unit, I think that both of us were expecting smart accommodation. What a disappointment! The place looked a dump and to make matters worse it was raining.

'Surely driver,' I said. 'This is not the Glider Pilot Headquarters?'

'Yes it is sir. It is called Tilshead and I think that you should now de-bus.'

Getting down, Norman and I surveyed our future home which consisted of 20 rather ancient wooden huts set out on either side of a parade ground. At one end was the Administrative block, whilst the largest building, making up the square, was the NAAFI. My first impression was one of bleak utilitarianism, devoid of character except for a tall white flagpole from which drooped the Regimental flag.

'Bugger me,' exclaimed Norman, 'what have we joined – a penal unit? It certainly looks grim.'

Fortunately, our dismal thoughts were interrupted by the arrival of a bright and cheerful little Captain who was accompanied by two very smart Sergeant-Majors from the Guards Regiment. 'OK chaps,' he called out, 'just leave your kit in the trucks and let's get the Hell out of this rain and into the NAAFI over there.' With that he turned and with a 'follow me', doubled towards the building followed by the rest of us. We entered a brightly lit room with easy chairs and tables dotted around, and a small stage and movie screen at one end.

'Sorry about the rain, our welcome is usually sunny. I am the Adjutant and I have organised tea and buns for you, so when you have taken off your wet coats, come and grab and make yourselves comfortable. The Commanding Officer, Col George Chatterton, will want to greet you officially in about a quarter of an hour.'

After Norman and I had collected 'tea and wads' we found a table near the front and sat down with a couple of other chaps.

'This is better,' I commented, 'here at least is a friendly atmosphere. I have heard quite a bit about the "chief" and look forward to meeting him.'

I had hardly spoken when the Adjutant called us to attention whilst a very smart looking officer, wearing a purple beret with badge and with RAF wings on his battle dress, strode in and jumped up onto the stage. About 5ft 8in tall, he stood looking at us for a moment and then said:

> 'Please sit down. My name is George Chatterton and I am the Commanding Officer of the Glider Pilot Regiment. You are all volunteers and, at this moment in time, have no idea of what you are letting yourselves in for! Well, the Glider Pilot Regiment is part of the Army Air Corps and will have the honour of delivering men, guns, vehicles and even tanks right into the very heart of the forthcoming battle. We will operate with the Airborne Divisions but, more specifically, with the Airlanding Brigades.
>
> 'Now, the great merit of using gliders is that large numbers of men and equipment arrive in bulk with pin-point accuracy and are immediately ready to fight. This then will be your job and in it, you will be unique because you will not only have to be a top rate pilot, but also able to fight efficiently after landing. You will be taught to fly whilst, at the same time, master every type of weapon and vehicle. Associated with your training you must develop the highest form of personal discipline and in this context I now introduce you to Sergeant-Majors Broidy and Cowlie of the Brigade of Guards who will be responsible for moulding us all into one proud unit, the smartest and most competent regiment in the Airborne forces.
>
> 'With discipline comes mental and physical fitness and you will find that the next few weeks will tax your strength and moral courage to the limit . . . I wish you success.'

After he had left, the Adjutant read out our hut numbers and gave details of meal times and the following day's parades. As it had stopped raining, Norman and I collected our kit and made our way to the Officer's block where we found a batman who fixed us up with a double room and, whilst helping unpack, put us in the picture about our training periods. It seemed that our days would consist of 'square bashing', physical training and route marches with a lecture or film on most evenings before supper.

'You are in for a hard time, sirs,' was the parting comment, 'but the Colonel expects the very best and anyone who fails to make the grade, is returned to his Regiment.' Whilst listening, my mind went back to the Tank Hunting Unit where I had insisted upon discipline, smartness and fitness and because I supported this policy, I suppose that I entered in the 'preliminary training' with enthusiasm. Fortunately I was extremely fit and, as I had been one of the Buckingham Palace Guard when the Honourable Artillery Company were given the honour during their 400th Anniversary, I had drilled every evening for weeks under the watchful eye of the Grenadier

Guard's RSM. Accordingly, 'square bashing' presented no hardship.

One problem I had was the fact that I was due to be married and to take off on a short honeymoon in September. When I explained to George Chatterton that I had been granted leave from my previous unit, his immediate response was:

'Of course John, you must get away. You are not due for flying yet and it would fit in nicely. You say that you are to be married in Aldwick Bay on Saturday the 5th. Well I live in Midhurst which is not far away and suggest that I give you your first Tiger Moth flight to Tangmere Aerodrome on the Friday afternoon. What do you say?'

'That would be wonderful Colonel. Thanks a million.'

'Furthermore, whilst I cannot give you your rank back yet, I would like you to accept a Glider Pilot beret with badge as a present. A little early perhaps, but I gather that you are doing well.'

'Thank you Colonel, I shall wear it with pride.'

Whilst my RAF log-book faithfully records my various flights, the fact that I took over the controls on that first trip has been entered as 'Introduction to Flying'.

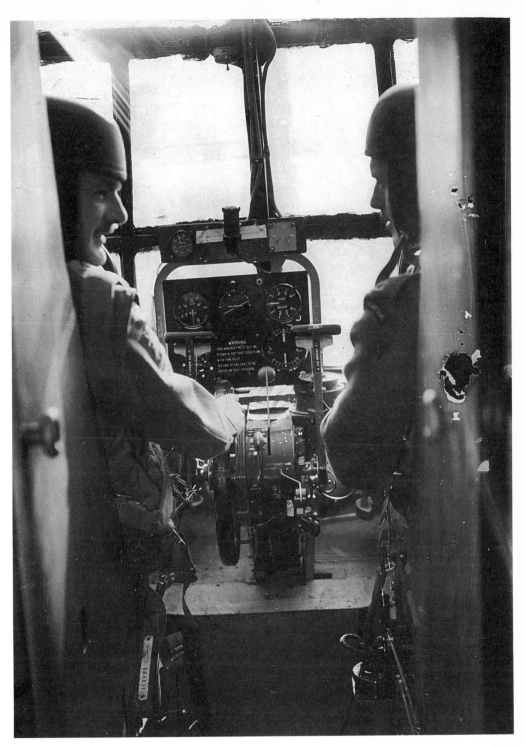

The author, on the left, at the controls of a glider.

The all-wood Airspeed Hotspur was used extensively for training in the Glider Pilot Regiment and was the first transport glider produced by the Allies in World War II. It carried two pilots, who boarded via the hinged Plexiglass canopy, and seven troops who entered via side doors. These two were photographed in 1940 having cut loose from their two aircraft. The Hotspur was never used in combat. *(Imperial War Museum; CM6030)*

TWO

FLYING TRAINING

Elementary Flying Training School (EFTS) – RAF Booker

On 20 September, I was posted to RAF Station Booker which is a fairly small aerodrome located a few miles from High Wycombe, north-west of London. It had previously been a flying club with a grass field and was now used to provide initial instruction to potential pilots. We were given the full RAF Elementary Training, including Navigation and Signalling.

There were four Flights of Tiger Moth and Miles Magister aircraft and because I was the Officer on our course, I was taken under the wing of a senior Squadron Leader who was a perfectionist, both strict and demanding with his tuition. Communication between the instructor and his pupil was by means of a rubber tube to earphones in the flying helmet and, in my case, it was a constant nagging of correction.

'You are flying right wing down Morrison. OK that's better but you have wandered 5 degrees off your compass bearing.'

'After a loop Morrison, you should still be on your original course and speed . . . Where are you off to now?'

'That slow roll was clumsy Morrison. You can do better than that. Look, I will show you again. Now have another go.'

In retrospect, I am grateful he was so demanding because he made me a better pilot, but I must confess that I was envious of some of my associates who had fun with the younger instructors. A change came when my Squadron Leader went sick with flu and I asked Flight Sergeant Needham if he would take me on. He had the reputation of being a good instructor but a bit of a dare-devil and, from the moment I started with him, my flying took on a completely fresh aspect.

My first 'lesson' was flying upside-down with me holding onto the cockpit sides like grim death because I had not fastened my straps tightly enough! We beat up clouds, had mock battles with another Tiger Moth and once, when on a low flying exercise, we dived down

17

into a railway cutting to meet a train steaming in the opposite direction. It was great, and I was quite disappointed when the Flight Commander returned. In the end the Chief Instructor gave me a good rating on my final test and I received my wings.

However, right at the end of the course, I had an experience which will always remain in my memory as proof that God decided to rescue me. It was the occasion of my last cross-country trip in a Miles Magister and I set course for Coventry aerodrome on a 55-minute flight. All went well and I duly booked in at the Control Tower to meet up with the Met. Officer. He gave me a weather forecast of light clouds building up from the south but assured me they would present no problem if I took off immediately. So, having calculated my return course, I received clearance from the Duty Officer and was on my way.

It was a lovely day, the sun was shining and, flying at 2000 feet, I was able to follow my route despite the scattered clouds below. I was feeling great and singing to myself, and I suppose my over-confidence was the start of my problem, because I suddenly realised that there was now a carpet of clouds below. 'Never mind,' I thought, 'this is probably only a patch over high hills and I will soon be able to see the ground once more.' However, after five more minutes of flying, it was ten-tenths cover and, looking behind, it seemed to be the same. I was now in trouble! A more experienced flyer would have turned north and scuttled back to Coventry but I was not all that far from home and wrongly assumed that the fine day 'up top' would soon give me a break in the clouds. How wrong I was.

Looking at the map, I could see that I was over low ground and therefore decided to descend slowly through the cloud and fly back to Booker at 500 feet. So, reducing speed, I brought the Magister down to the top of the cloud formation and, holding my breath, continued into the murky surroundings. By now the windscreen was opaque and I could hardly see my way in the grey mist. Still no break and my altimeter was showing 600 feet!

In fear and trepidation, I dropped further when suddenly I could see vaguely through the cloud and, to my horror, realised that I was right over a village with a church tower 200 yards in front. How I missed it I do not know, but in my panic, I pushed on full throttle and climbed steeply into the sunshine once more. Thank God I was alive, but what ever was I to do now?

Right throughout the trip I had maintained course and calculated I was 5 minutes from Booker. If the cloud was down to ground level, there was no hope of landing and equally, I was not prepared to bale out and allow my aircraft to crash into a built-up area. I therefore decided to continue flying towards the coast which was about 60 miles away, in the hope that I could get down to sea level and approach land

18

from the south. My engine was running sweetly. I had plenty of fuel and I prayed. How I prayed! As if in answer to my call for help, a miracle happened for, away to the right, a small gap in the cloud cover opened up and when I made my way over to it, I saw a white concrete road that I recognised as part of the housing estate which bordered onto the airfield. Happily, I dropped through the gap and completed the circuit to land at Booker which had actually been closed down.

For a full minute I sat silently thanking the Almighty and then slowly taxied towards my Flight hut to be greeted by Needham.

'Where the hell have you been? Giving the girls in Coventry a good time? We thought we had lost you.'

'You nearly did,' I replied, unhooking my seat straps and clambering wearily out of the cockpit. Then it all came out.

'You were a bloody fool,' came the well earned comment. 'Directly it started to close in, you should have gone back. You were darned lucky my boy . . . someone up there must have been looking after you!'

He certainly was.

Light Glider Training – RAF Croughton

My next posting was RAF Croughton where I was introduced to gliders in the form of the Hotspur, a beautifully proportioned low wing monoplane produced by General Aircraft. The instructor and pupil sat in tandem and, operationally, the glider would carry eight fully-equipped soldiers.

For my first lesson I was in the care of Sgt Moran who explained the aircraft controls in detail before climbing in and securing the glider's cockpit cover. In the meantime, a Harvard aircraft tug had taken up its position ahead of us on the runway and the tow rope connected.

'Right,' said Moran, 'this time I will take off and land, but, before handing the controls over to you I will first show you the ideal position both in the high and low tow stations. OK? Well here we go.' As he spoke, the tug started to surge forward with the glider in tow.

'First we have to assist the tug by reducing the ground drag and so we become airborne as soon as possible. I do this by gently easing back on the stick and hold the glider a few feet above the runway. When the tug has sufficient speed, it will take off and we follow it up as it climbs, holding station slightly above it. This gives him the ideal "pull" and as he starts to turn away from the aerodrome we just follow him. OK? Over to you . . . you now have the controls.'

'Roger,' I replied, 'I've got her.' And with excitement, I applied slight pressure on the rudder bar with my feet and gently moved the control stick to activate the elevator and ailerons. My first impression was that the Hotspur was much lighter to handle than the Tiger Moth. It tended to float out of position but otherwise it was easy to handle.

'OK,' came the comment. 'You seem to have mastered the high tow position. I will now show you the low tow. I've got her.' With that, he took over the controls and moved the glider through the slipstream down to a station just below the tug. 'This station is used when flying in cloud as it is easier to distinguish the silhouette of the tug from under looking up. OK? You take over.'

'Roger, I've got her,' and experienced no difficulty in holding station.

'OK? Now take her up slowly to the high tow station.'

Moving the stick back, I felt the glider gain height and the view of the tug changed as we moved to stay just above it.

'That was good but remember always to take it slowly when changing position.

'Now we have just about completed a wide circuit of the aerodrome and you will see that we are cross wind and about 4 miles away. I will take over and land. First I release the tow by pulling this lever.'

As he did so, there was a loud 'clunk' and I could see the tow rope whipping behind the tug as it climbed away to the starboard, but the most impressive sensation was the complete silence that prevailed. The noise of the slipstream had suddenly disappeared and we seemed to be suspended like a huge bird in the heavens. Moran then swooped the Hotspur first to the left, then to the right and when I took over the controls there was a wonderful feeling of freedom. Indeed, I wished that we could have stayed up for ever. However, my instructor had other ideas and with an 'OK I've got her' started to make the approach.

'First,' he said, 'I reduce speed by raising the nose of the glider and then lift this lever which forces down the flaps to slow us still further. A steady turn to port brings us into line with the runway and you will see that we are losing height all the time to cross the perimeter fence about 300 feet up which is just right for a perfect landing.' So it was, for we floated down to skim above the tarmac and for the wheels to make contact and gently bring us to a halt.

'There you are,' laughed Moran. 'What do you think of gliding?'

'Quite wonderful,' I enthused.

'Well, we have got a couple of more circuits to do and this time you can try your hand. Don't worry, I shall be here with the master controls and if you get into trouble, just let go!'

Whilst he was speaking, the towing aircraft taxied onto the runway ahead of us and the ground crew hitched it up to us.

'Are you ready? Well it's over to you, so give them the thumbs-up sign.'

'Here we go,' I thought as the Harvard gathered speed and my glider lifted off, perhaps a little high but then, when the tug became airborne, I was able to follow him quite easily. The circuit went well and when we reached the release point Moran came on, 'OK, I now want you to "pull the plug" and start your descent. Take it easy.'

Reducing speed, I put on the flaps but turned early and had to apply right rudder to bring the glider back in line with the runway.

'You were in too much of a hurry to get down,' chipped in Moran, 'and as a result, will be a little high over the fence. Never mind, just carry on and land her.'

I duly flattened out above the tarmac and proudly assumed a good landing only to realise that I was 6 feet up and the Hotspur was still flying happily. My initial reaction was to push the controls forward and this, of course, resulted in a fancy bounce after which I was then 3 feet up! Eventually, she lost speed and sank gratefully to the ground.

'Well, we are down,' chortled Moran. 'A little rough perhaps, but down. I can tell you that this happens with nine out of ten "first land-ings". Just remember that your glider will take its time to settle, so hold her until you feel that she is losing flying speed and then ease the controls forward and she will stick. OK, let's see if we can do better next time.'

I was soon airborne once again and this time the tug took us up wider and a 1000 foot higher and, guided by my instructor, I enjoyed the thrill of free flight, zooming around in circles until eventually, it was time to land. Fortunately my effort on this occasion was successful and we touched down gently to run forward a few yards.

'Well done,' came the comment. 'That was a good landing. Keep them all like it! Hop out now as I have some more pilots to take up. Provided that the weather holds, I shall see you tomorrow.'

I made my way back to the Flight Office absolutely elated with the experience and sat down to watch, with a smug grin, the 'bumps' of some of my associates. During that week, I had four more trips with other instructors and was then allowed to go solo to practise take-offs and landings. Thereafter the course followed the general pattern of EFTS (but without aerobatics in gliders) and I was able to scrounge quite a few hours in the Flight's Tiger Moth. The Station Commander encouraged us to team up on cross-countrys and I became great friends with Andy Andrews who was later to become the Regiment's Operations Officer. I firmly believe that our close association was instrumental in my collecting all sorts of jobs in the belief that 'John Morrison is just the chap for that!'

Heavy Glider Training – RAF Brize Norton

I was transferred to the Heavy Gliding Conversion Unit in October 1943 and was based at Brize Norton which was a pre-war regular airforce station well equipped with excellent accommodation and all other facilities. It was now operating with Whitley bombers and was mainly responsible for the training of parachutists and pilots for conversion to the Horsa glider.

The Horsa was a vastly different glider from the little Hotspur in that it was probably four times its size and had a wingspan wider than the bombers that towed it. Made completely of wood, it could carry a load of up to three-and-a-half tons and was designed to deliver 28 fully-equipped men, or a jeep with gun, right to the forefront of the battle. Its total weight, fully loaded, amounted to nearly eight tons which was quite a haul for a two-engine aircraft like the Whitley. The first and second pilots sat in a roomy Perspex cockpit which provided all-round vision. Each had a spade grip control column and, on the panel in front of them, there was a height and airspeed indicator and a compass. The actual tow was made with a 150 yard hemp rope that bifurcated short of the glider to attach to the leading edges of each wing with a special quick-release fitting.

My training followed the previous procedures of circuits and landings but with greater concentration on night flying when, at a later stage, we used only five goose-neck flares to provide indications of wind direction and height of ground. Being a much larger aircraft, it required a greater degree of physical handling and, to some extent, prompt anticipation of any changes by the tug as it was slower to respond.

The greatest difference in the flying is during the descent where, in action, the pilot wants to get down to ground level as soon as possible. Therefore, having released the tow rope, he immediately reduces speed and pulls back a lever to bring down the very large barn door type flaps. Then, pushing the spade control column right forward, he aims the Horsa straight down just short of the front boundary of the landing zone and experiences the strange phenomenon of seeing the ground appearing to come right up to him at a steady 85 mph. Depending where his glider is required to finish, he flattens out and sinks to the ground to run up to the desired spot.

Once again I satisfied the Chief Instructor that I was competent and was posted as a Flight Commander in 'D' Squadron.

THREE

PREPARING FOR THE INVASION

RAF Stoney Cross

By now the Regiment was growing rapidly. No 1 Wing was in Italy, under the command of the First Airborne Division, whilst No 2 Wing, of which I was a member, already had three Squadrons each consisting of three Flights. I now commanded No 5 Flight which had 4 Officers and 40 Sergeant or Staff Sergeant pilots and, assuming that we were carrying only infantry, was capable of lifting a Battalion complete with their jeeps and mortars.

Our first operational posting was to a bomber squadron based at Stoney Cross which is a medium-sized station about 15 miles from the south coast. We were only there for a month, during which time I was able to persuade the Station Commander to give my crews night flying. It followed that most of my evenings were spent on the Glider Runway, watching take-offs and the safe return of my 'flock'. Perhaps the most memorable event was the cross-country trip made by Staff Sgt Tommy Tomkins and to explain, I quote from his subsequent report.

'Our take-off and climb went well but, somehow, the intercom leads between the tug and glider must have broken, because after 15 minutes we lost verbal contact. Anyway, we continued and the tug levelled out at 3000 feet where we encountered slight cloud. This didn't worry me at first but, it wasn't long before I experienced the greatest difficulty in picking out the lights on the wing tips of the towing aircraft and to hold the correct station. It then started to rain and obviously the tug pilot decided to abort the exercise because he slowly made a wide turn back towards the aerodrome.

'Shortly afterwards, my second pilot noticed that the rear gunner in the bomber was signalling with a torch. It certainly wasn't Morse and so I assumed that he was telling me that the aerodrome was below and that I should release the tow when ready. Looking down, I could now see the runway lights and so pulled off and we were free. We had plenty of height to glide homewards, but it was only when we were cross wind and ready for the final approach that I was conscious that something was wrong. The runway lights seemed to be whiter and blinking but, as it was raining, I assumed that this was the reason. However as we approached the front limit lights and flattened to touch down, I saw water! Somehow, I was landing on water!

'Then everything happened at once. When my wheels made contact, the front of the glider crashed down to hit the surface with a tremendous splash and we seemed to plunge into the waves before finally surfacing with water pouring into the cockpit. Quickly releasing our straps, we made our way back to the upper hatch and bashed it open to climb through onto the wing and there we sat shouting for help as our glider steadily settled. We were obviously not out to sea as there were no waves and must have come down into Poole Harbour. Indeed this proved to be the case when, after 20 minutes, we were rescued by a motor-boat and told that we had landed on the Catalina Flying Boat strip and, by so doing, had delayed the take-off! The Fleet Air Arm thought that it was the funniest landing that they had ever seen and they certainly looked after us.'

In the meantime the tug pilot had reported that the glider had released the tow early and had turned away from Stoney Cross. I didn't sleep that night, having warned all the authorities to expect a glider crash and it was only next morning that I received the glad news that the pilots were safe. The glider itself was towed ashore, taken to bits and transported back home happily, but the paper work kept me busy for a week.

RAF Keevil

On 1 January, my Flight (No 5 Flight) took off in our Horsa gliders to fly to what was to be our permanent base at Keevil. Due to a change in policy, the glider flights were attached to the RAF units that were to tow us and I had the great pleasure of flying as part of Squadron Leader David Davies' crew. We all became the greatest of friends and on the intercom we were known as Numbers 7 and 8.

They had just been equipped with Stirling aircraft, the powerful four-engine bomber which, due to problems of flying at the heights now required for bombing, had been transferred to No 38 Group. Indeed, when these Stirlings were equipped for towing, it was rumoured that, as the glider moved through the considerable slipstream to the 'low tow' position, its tail might fall off! As explained earlier,this manoeuvre was employed when flying through cloud where losing sight of the tug could result in serious consequences. However, with the towing aircraft above him, the glider pilot could use a device called the 'Angle of Dangle' which gave a rough indication of where the tug should be. The 'low tow' position was also used to enable the rear gunner of a Stirling to fight off a stern attack.

As we were to be the first 'operational flight' to fly behind the Stirling, it was vital that both the RAF and Glider Pilot crews should be free of any misgivings about the performance of the combination in action. Accordingly, I approached my tug pilot, Squadron Leader Davies.

'Davie,' I said, 'there is a rumour going around that there is a problem with the glider moving down from the high to the low tow position. Have you heard it?'

'No, and I find it difficult to believe. After all, they must have carried out full trials. Although, I suppose that this is a manoeuvre only used in special operational circumstances. Well there is only one way to find out. Can you arrange for a dummy load and we will have a shot at it tomorrow morning. It might also be a good opportunity to experiment with some ideas I have on evasive action should the combination be attacked by a fighter.'

I think that we all realised that any tug with a glider on tow would be a sitting duck for an enemy fighter and that, in the event of an attack, would have no option but to cast off the tow to defend itself. The 'Skipper' was now suggesting that the combination should first try to carry out simple evasive action which, due to its slow speed, might cause the fighter to overshoot and give the Stirling gunners the opportunity to shoot back. Once again, as this would impose additional stress on the tug, tow-rope and glider, a trial was warranted and so, next morning, having first established the sequence of the manoeuvres, I and my second pilot duly took our places in the cockpit of a loaded glider and with some apprehension, gave the thumbs-up sign to the RAF ground crew to show that we were ready. A click in my earphones told me that 'Matchbox', as we were called, was now connected into the intercom circuit of the tug and I could hear Davie running through the pre-take-off checks with his crew. Finally it was our turn.

'Hello Matchbox, are you all set?'

'Yes No 1,' I replied. 'Could we try four runs through the slipstream first?'

'As many as you like Matchbox, until you are happy. I think that we will climb and circuit the aerodrome at 5000 feet so that, if we do part company, you can land safely.'

'Roger No 1, we are ready to roll.' Switching off my mike, I grinned at Wally Beech. 'I hope that they realise that we do not have parachutes because I have never flown a glider without a tail.'

Basically, the secret of a comfortable flight is for the tug to have a straight pull. If the glider is too high, the tug's tail is lifted and the pilot has to trim to counter. Or if the glider wanders to one side, it imposes a strain on the tug which will tend to yaw. It follows that these considerations were vital during our evasion exercise and I had to be meticulous in keeping station.

When we reached the desired altitude, I called up the Skipper. 'No 1, this is No 7. OK if I now change to the low tow station?'

'Sure. Go ahead.'

I slowly eased the column forward. At first nothing seemed to happen except the silhouette of the tug changed as we flew right behind, but as we dropped further, I was conscious of increased vibration on the controls and a considerable rise in wind noise. The lower our station, the more pronounced this became and our glider was really shuddering as if subjected to a hurricane, but as quickly as it started, so the noise suddenly stopped and I levelled off to fly just below the slipstream to look up at the underbelly of the Stirling. So far, so good, I quietly tried my elevators and rudder and, when satisfied that all was well, again called up.

'No 1 this is Matchbox, we are still with you. What about changing back to the high tow position.'

'OK Matchbox go ahead.'

I then reversed the procedure and after a similar buffeting, resumed station above the tug.

'OK No 1. I would like the Second Pilot to do the next one and then, we will do one more each way but a little faster.'

'Roger Matchbox. When you are ready.'

All went well, except that on the last change upwards, I deliberately pulled back strongly to emulate an emergency change, but having failed to correct quickly enough, I finished far too high and pulled the Stirling's tail right up.

'Sorry No 1, I won't try that again.'

'All right you clown,' came the reply, 'but give us warning next time you want to take over the tow! Are you ready now for ACTION RIGHT?'

In this manoeuvre, the tug makes a climbing turn to the right and then drops down, changing direction 90 degrees. I suppose that it could be considered as a stall turn but under power and my problem was to keep station. Directly I saw the Stirling starting the starboard climb, I pulled back on the column and applied right bank and rudder, but the glider was heavy and cumbersome and I really had to heave on the controls to prevent the forward impetus from taking us outside the course of the tug. I had hardly done this before the Stirling dropped away and I immediately shoved the column forward with right rudder to follow him down. It was like handling a barge, for our change of direction was so slow that only panic correction prevented the glider

26

from pulling the tug out of the sky.

'Not so hot Matchbox,' came the terse comment. 'Let's try again. ACTION RIGHT.' This time I anticipated the Stirling and nearly turned inside the flight path but the end result was smoother and by the third attempt was 'bang on'.

'OK ACTION LEFT.' We then completed the same exercise the other way.

Whilst we were battling, I could see the rear gunner assuming fighter attacks from various angles so that after 30 minutes of 'avoiding action' we were all pretty exhausted. Even so, it was worthwhile for, apart from becoming a true member of the tug crew, I gained the experience of manhandling a large and heavy glider with the smug satisfaction that I never lost a tail.

Mass Landings and Battle Training

During the three months preceding D-Day, No 5 Flight took part in six mass landings, one of the earliest, being on an American Airfield at Welford where 97 gliders, comprising Horsas and American Wacos were employed. It was my first experience of Yankee Glider Pilots and I was amazed at the dare-devil techniques they used. Admittedly the Waco is a much smaller and lighter aircraft, but they approached the landing zone at all heights and from every direction, simply dumping them down in a cloud of dust. Strangely enough, not a soul was hurt, but the post-flight maintenance would have been quite considerable.

It was an afternoon exercise and the plan was for the Horsa gliders to depart immediately and before the Dakota tugs landed, but the Yanks had other ideas. 'No lousy Limey is going to make me late for my date!' The whole squadron arrived *en masse* completely disregarding the red Very lights warning that the runway was already occupied by gliders and Stirling aircraft. The outcome was that half of my Flight failed to take off that evening and I enjoyed the generous hospitality at their canteen.

Whilst night flying was now our priority, we obviously had to take our turn with our RAF Squadron's own programme which gave me the chance of giving battle training to my pilots. My guess was that at least 80% of the chaps had never been under fire, nor had fired a shot in anger, and so I made a point of getting to know the old officer who was in charge of the field-firing range about 10 miles away. I planned various exercises there using live ammunition and explosives and it obviously paid dividends for, in action, the pilots were understandably alarmed but not frightened.

27

Indeed, the only casualty we had was a 'civilian' electrician who collected a ricochet bullet in his backside. Everyone had been warned to stay clear of the area and red flags were plentiful, but it seems that he was up a tree wiring 'perimeter lighting' for the nearby airfield and stayed there to watch. The first that I knew of the problem was the sight of a tree surrendering with a white handkerchief! I had to stop the exercise to take him to the local Station Doctor who cauterised the abrasion. After reporting the incident, I forgot all about it, but not so 'our friend'. Twenty months later I received a summons for two weeks wages and a new pair of trousers.

I suppose the climax to our night flying exercises was the mass landing at Netheravon Airfield. The plan was for the Independent Parachute Unit to land first to set out a short flarepath in the form of a 'T' with the stem pointing into the wind. About 150 gliders were then to fly into pre-arranged sections of the field. When we had the 'flight' briefing at Keevil, the Squadron Navigation Officer explained that, as the wind was presently blowing from the south, the tugs would bring the gliders crosswind to the north of the airfield and the landing would be from north to south. We all set off happily on a beautiful evening but, unknown to us, the wind must have changed during our cross-country flight and the flarepath was laid out for landing south to north.

'Hello there Matchbox,' came the worried call from the Skipper. 'Something is adrift here. We are on the wrong end of the flarepath, so I had better take you round again.'

'OK No 1 'I replied,' it looks as if there has been a 'cock-up' somewhere. Could the wind have changed in the last hour or so?'

'Possibly No 7. Everything is now "arse-about-front".'

'Well the rule is that we must land in the direction shown by the flarepath, so I am going to comply.' Turning to my second pilot I said, 'OK Beech old chap, give me full flap' and with that, we started our descent to turn onto the flarepath. But calamity!

'Christ, sir,' shouted Beech, 'they are landing in the opposite direction. Look out, a Horsa is going to hit us.' Sure enough there was a dark shadow heading straight for us but luckily, I was able to heave back on the controls and we had sufficient speed to pull up over him. However, by so doing, my aircraft then started to stall and I had to shove the spade grip right forward. We hit the ground with an awful thump and I was apprehensive that my undercarriage had collapsed, but all was well and I ran up to our pre-determined position to apply the brakes with a sigh of relief.

'We were bloody lucky there Beech. Come on, let's get the Hell out of here before someone lands on us.' Hurriedly pulling open the side panel, we both jumped down and ran a few yards away to stand watching the ensuing shambles. Gliders were landing in all directions and the subsequent sounds of tearing wood and smashed wings provided a sad memory that I will never forget. For a while, the mêlée continued and then there was silence, except for the cries for help from injured pilots.

The official report states that there were no collisions and no fatalities! I suppose we have to be grateful we were not carrying troops and that the tragedy, bad as it was, produced very definite rules of procedure for future operations.

Preliminary Top Secret Briefing

As May came, we were all very conscious of the impending invasion and that we would be the spearhead of the airborne attack. Whilst the full plans were known to but a few, Colonel George Chatterton was called in for a personal briefing by Major-General Gale, Commander of the 6th Airborne Division and told that three Brigades would be 'landing' east of the British beaches in Normandy during the night before the seaborne invasion. They had the major task of protecting the left flank against the probable German counter-attack.

In this initial assault, the Glider Pilot Regiment was given two objectives, both of which were vital. The first was to land three gliders on or near a battery of 6-inch guns at Merville that were sited to fire down the beaches. The emplacements themselves were heavily armoured and surrounded by a moat full of mines and, unless neutralised, the guns would create havoc with the landing craft. To achieve this, the gliders were to be towed by Halifax bombers at 4000 feet and released just short of the coast when they were to navigate in darkness and crashland by the German battery. Certainly a formidable undertaking! To assist them, they were to use a secret homing device called 'Rebecca' that matched onto a similar unit carried by a parachutist who was to be dropped earlier. Upon landing, the troops carried were to assault and capture the guns.

The second task was to deliver a company of the Oxfordshire and Buckinghamshire Light Infantry Regiment into two small fields adjacent to the bridges over the Caen Canal and the River Orne. They would then assault, capture and hold them at all cost until the arrival of a Commando unit that would land by sea later on the following morning. Again the gliders would have to navigate in darkness some 7 miles inland and the pilots themselves fight with the unit.

Upon receipt of his orders, Col Chatterton chose the crews for special training at locations similar to those on which they would have to land, and at the same time stepped up practice night landings for other Squadrons.

The next step towards our part in the invasion came on 3 June when

Squadron Commanders and certain Flight Officers received a summons to attend a special briefing at RAF Netheravon. Once cleared by 'security', we were escorted to a shed on site, where we were again checked by a Glider Pilot Major before entering a brightly lit room and there, for the first time, I realised our destination was Normandy. It was represented by a huge model of the beach front and surrounding areas and showed every landmark such as hotels, church spires, village squares, water towers, ponds etc. so that, once our approach lines were established, it would be possible to anticipate exactly what we would see on the flight to our landing zone. It was a complete revelation and we all clustered excitedly around the model until called to order by the Operations Officer.

> 'Well chaps,' he said pointing to the display, 'this is it! Normandy. I will first give you details of the Master Plan, the objectives of the 6th Airborne Division and finally the tasks of our Squadrons.' Using a pointer, he briefly sketched the invasion strategy with the British and American forces landing on five beaches to the north of Caen.
>
> 'The 6th Airborne Division will land east of the River Orne, on D–1, to hold the left flank of the British "Sword" beach and to fight off the anticipated German counter-attacks until the arrival of the 51st Division by sea. This is a tremendous responsibility and it is essential that the elements of the Airlanding Brigade are safely delivered by us exactly as required.'

He then listed the various glider objectives during the night of D–1 and also on D-Day which included the mass lift of 7000 men with their equipment and supporting arms. We were part of this operation and D Squadron were to deliver two companies of the 'Ox & Bucks' together with artillery into a landing zone to the south of the village of Ranville at 2100 hrs.

> 'Glider pilots will fight with the troops that they carry but as the Master Plan envisages a second phase when the 1st Airborne Division will land beyond Caen, once that city has been occupied, you will be needed back at your RAF stations for the next lift. Therefore, expect to be instructed to make your way to the beach where you will embark on a landing craft returning to England.'

Pausing for a minute to allow us to digest the briefing so far, the Operations Officer continued.

> 'I now want to dwell on the flight plan. The model in front of you is an accurate reproduction of your landing zones. You will see grid lines on

it and also the planned approach routes of each RAF Squadron. The 'boffins' in 38 Group have produced a film of the proposed journey taken by an overhead camera using a blue filter, that will give aircrews and Glider Pilots a picture of what they should see when crossing the coast right down to the final approach. This will be shown during the final briefing.

'The landing zone for the mass delivery of the Airlanding Brigade in the evening is clearly defined on the model. On the ground, the Independent Parachute Unit will mark the direction of the wind with smoke and pilots will decide when to release in order to finish up at their pre-planned locations.

'All very well, but we do have a major problem. Poles! Last month, one of our reconnaissance aircraft came up with a photograph showing a large number of white dots in fields by the coast which were recognised as holes dug to accommodate anti-glider poles. Later, when these were planted by the Germans, they were found to be 20 feet tall and about two feet in diameter. A formidable obstruction. Accordingly, an immediate decision was made to drop Royal Engineer parachutists first with the task of blasting down these poles if possible in lines, but in the battle, this may not happen, so be aware of the problem and avoid them.'

After a general discussion, the lights were turned down and we were shown the film of the approach which was quite fantastic. The Operations Officer continued:

'One final instruction, you are to maintain complete and absolute security. All personnel will be confined to the station, no telephone calls, and no communication outside. You will not brief your pilots until instructed to do so. All clear . . . well good luck.'

Elated and excited, I made my way back to Keevil where I found that the troops that we were to carry had set up tents in the corner of the airfield. In the Flight itself, the chaps were obviously anticipating action, but in view of security clamp, all that I could tell them was that air and seaborne landings were to take place shortly but that the time and destination would only be revealed at the final briefing. In the meantime, weapons and equipment were to be checked and those wishing to write letters should hand them to Flight Headquarters for posting after take-off.

FOUR

OPERATION *OVERLORD* – NORMANDY

Crew Briefing

It was still dark when I awoke on the morning of 6 June and I was conscious of a tremendous feeling of excitement that, after so much training, we were at last going into battle. I wondered how No 5 Flight would perform and, more specifically, how I would fare during the onslaught. One thing was certain, we had prepared ourselves completely both as pilots and fighters and the *esprit de corps* within the unit was quite outstanding.

I had called for a Flight parade at 8.30 a.m. in order to tidy up and check weapons before making our way over to the RAF briefing hut where we broke up to join our respective tug crews.

'Ah, here come the cavalry,' called out Davie. 'The invasion has really started!'

'Dead right Skipper,' I replied, 'and we are raring to go. By the way, is there any news of the parachute drop or the special glider landings last night?'

'I haven't heard anything, except that they were delivered correctly and on time by the Halifax tugs that were used to give them the additional height. We have been told that the sea landings on the British beaches met with heavy opposition but are progressing according to schedule.'

The crew briefing concentrated on the routes to be followed and details of the weather and at the end, the famous film was run through three times.

'Well,' commented Davie, 'we shouldn't have difficulty finding our way. The main problem as I see it will be flak when we cross the coast as it will still be daylight. Then you chaps still have to avoid any poles that may still be around. Don't worry, I am sure that everything will be fine. Look after yourselves and good luck.'

Afterwards, we sat around looking at routes on the maps and it was only then that I realised that our particular stream left the English coast at Bognor, my home town! Turning to my second pilot I said, 'Wally, once we are airborne, you will fly the glider so I can see my house and wave goodbye. Keep a firm hold on the tow-release lever just in case I am tempted! There is nothing more to do at present, so I am going to buy the crew a beer, have a quick lunch and I will see you at the Flight at 2 o'clock.'

Because the pilots were now fully briefed and prepared, I handed over to the Section Officers to get their men to the tow-path in plenty of time whilst I pushed off to my room to check and load my revolver and prime the grenades that I carried. Then I made my way down to see how No 4 Flight were getting on with loading the jeeps, trailers and guns of the Anti-tank Battery.

As both the gunners and our infantry would be operating on the far left flank, I took the opportunity of chatting to their commander as we strolled over to the van that was distributing tea and buns.

'You have collected a honey of a job preventing the Panzer Units from breaking through to the beach, that is, until the seaborne artillery arrives,' I remarked, 'and I wish you every success.'

'Yes, I am anticipating problems, but it's going to be a case of catching them by surprise, particularly if they try to move overnight. I am keeping my fingers crossed for fine weather tomorrow, because the promised support from fighters will weigh the scales in our favour. Anyway, the Ox & Bucks you are carrying are a grand bunch and will sort out the supporting German infantry.' Then, with a cheery wave of his bun, he went away to check on his gun crews.

I was still standing by the tea van when the Sections marched in, followed shortly by the Ox & Bucks companies. My pilots quickly found the platoons that they were to carry and within minutes were laughing and joking with them. Standing back, I felt it strange that, within a few hours, we would all be facing death and yet, there we were, cup in one hand and bun in the other, supremely confident of a successful outcome.

It was now 4 o'clock and the Glider Pilots were moving off with their passengers to settle the men strapped in on either side of the main body with their officer sitting nearest the cockpit. I left Staff Sergeant Beech to collect the Company Headquarters having first secured all loose items such as the wireless set and bicycle with straps to the floor. Whilst this was done, Major Farrell and I walked down the lines of gliders checking that they were all ready and, with a final warning to the pilots to watch for the poles and to finish well into the landing zone, I gave them the thumbs-up sign and returned to my glider.

On previous exercises, my flight was always off first and therefore, as No 1 glider, I used to observe the preparations and the approach of the leading Stirling aircraft. Now I had 22 gliders of No 4 Flight ahead of me and it seemed an age before it was our turn. However, there they came approaching steadily down the perimeter track and I could recognise Davie as he waved to us prior to moving via the feed-in lane onto the main runway ahead of my glider.

The ground crew quickly locked the towrope into the tail of the Stirling, after which there was a loud click in my earphones and a cheery voice called over, 'Hello Matchbox, hello Matchbox, are you receiving me?'

'Receiving you loud and clear No 1 and ready to go.'

'That's good. So what are we waiting for.' The tug took up the slack and opened up with all engines.

Flight and Landing

As my glider was lightly loaded, we became airborne within a short distance and thereafter I was able to hold station as the Stirling climbed. It was a cloudy, rather gusty day and initially I was concerned that we might have to move down to the low-tow station, but when we arrived at our 'cruising' height of 2500 feet, it cleared slightly. Already, there were a number of streams of aircraft from the various stations all heading eastwards, and soon the sky was full of tugs and gliders with a constant attendance of fighters weaving around above.

Keevil is 140 miles from the south coast and I was soon able to hand the controls over to Beech which enabled me to watch out for Bognor Pier and there it was, right on track. Glancing to the right, I could recognise the area of our house and happily waved to my wife who I was sure would be standing in the garden excited at the fantastic sight of 1500 aircraft. As it happened, by a strange quirk of fate, at that very moment she was in the hall of Bognor railway station waiting to pick up her father, and did not see the huge air armada.

Our journey took us across 150 miles of the Channel. Looking down I could make out the wash of hundreds of craft ploughing through fairly rough seas towards Normandy, whilst above and to the right were tugs and gliders flying steadily onward. I was relishing this memorable moment when the Skipper came through.

'Hello No 7, we seem to be on track and it won't be long before we can see the French coast. Is everything all right with you?'

'Yes thanks No 1. Those puffs of black smoke on the horizon . . . is that anti-aircraft fire?'

'Yes. It's what we expected but we will have to press on and hope for the best. Get Wally busy with his good luck charm!'

By now, to our right I could see Sword beach which seemed to be full of landing craft, many of them still flying barrage balloons, whilst the sand and beach approaches appeared completely churned up by tracked vehicles. Our approach was to the left of the River Orne and we could already recognise some of the larger houses that were highlighted for us on the film.

It all seemed to happen so quickly for next came the cheery comment. 'OK chaps, as you will be leaving us soon, we will say cheerio for now. Good luck. There will be a cold beer waiting for you when you get back.'

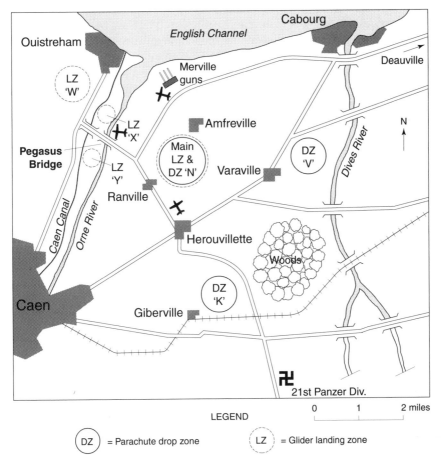

LEGEND

(DZ) = Parachute drop zone   (LZ) = Glider landing zone

LZ & DZ ASSIGNMENTS

LZ 'X' & 'Y' = Bridge attack troops   DZ 'K' = 8th Parachute Battalion

LZ 'W' = Glider troops (reinforcements)   DZ 'N' = 7th, 12th & 13th Parachute Battalions

Main LZ = 6th Air Landing Brigade   DZ 'V' = 1st Canadian & 9th Parachute Battalions

'Thanks No 1, I can see our landing area already. Thanks for the ride.' With that, I pulled the tow release lever and started to reduce speed.

I must confess that, whilst I was conscious of flak during our approach, the fact that someone was actually shooting at my glider was sharply brought home when I saw 'pom-pom' shells setting up a barrage ahead but, luckily for us, the German gunner switched to a Stirling following. Now I could see our field marked by purple smoke and decided to land as soon as possible.

'Quick Wally, it's too hot up here, let's get down. Give me half flap ... that's fine ... now full flap.' Thrusting the controls right forward, we hurtled in at speed, and there were the poles!

A hurried glance gave me the impression that they had been planted in lines and because we were further inland, the spacing was much wider and the lines were staggered. Therefore it was possible to make a 45-degree turn to approach diagonally, which I did to run up right to the top end of our field. However, because of my speed, the last 50 yards was one huge skid and the glider finished up with a resounding crash into an earth bank which jolted us somewhat but, fortunately, also provided welcome protection against the increasing volume of fire.

By the time Wally Beech and I had extricated ourselves, Major Farrell and his men had already pulled open the side door and jumped out to set up his Company HQ in the corner. Meanwhile, other gliders of the Flight were arriving and quite a few spotted my skid marks and followed the more suitable approach. Unfortunately, others collected the poles in their run up which meant the loss of a wing or undercarriage but no injury to the troops carried. However, one of my crews hit a pole head-on and the first pilot was killed instantly.

First Assault

The Germans were not taking our arrival quietly and, initially, we collected considerable rifle and machine-gun fire. However, as sometimes happens, this was directed at the gliders themselves. Once we had vacated them, we were relatively sheltered until they brought up the mortars which made life uncomfortable! The answer was a deep hole which Beech and I excavated in double-quick time.

By now, dusk had fallen and the Ox & Bucks platoons had taken up defensive positions. Whilst the German small-arms fire had stopped, the mortars, having successfully found the range, continued to plaster us. We could clearly identify where they were and Farrell ordered his reserve platoon to attack them from the flank. This they did and I was to follow our first assault from the sound of Sten-gun fire as they stormed in to capture the position. In fact, there was no opposition as it seems that the mortar crews had been left without any protection and they meekly surrendered, presenting us with three medium-size mortars, a number of bombs and ten prisoners who reluctantly carried their weapons back and set them up at Company HQ. During the evening, I heard our anti-tank guns in action and a fair amount of machine-gun fire around Ranville, but otherwise my first night in France was reasonably quiet.

In our briefing, we had been told that the German 21st Panzer Division was located further to the east of our position and that the anticipated armour counter-attack would first come from them. Accordingly when at 4 a.m. we could distinctly hear the sound of tracked vehicles, we realised that we were now 'for it' because a 45-ton Tiger Tank presents a formidable proposition! But miracles happen and this time we were saved by the Navy. Warned of the danger, an Army spotter plane was airborne at first light and located the squadrons of German tanks assembling for the attack. Fortunately, the pilot was in direct communication with the Navy who promptly alerted HMS *Warspite* which was standing offshore. After a couple of sighters, she let loose with tremendous shelling and heavily blasted the whole area.

It was a fantastic experience to witness the terrible fire power of this battleship and to hear the huge shells roaring overhead like express trains to land with devastating effect right on the German assembly. The carnage must have been appalling and the severely damaged tanks shortly abandoned their attack and retired to Caen.

During the afternoon of 7 June, the Commandos and units of the 51st Highland Division passed through our position and it was now clear that armour was well established ashore. I had taken the opportunity of visiting the various platoons with Major Farrell and noted how well the pilots had settled in with the infantry. They were all very 'full' of themselves. That evening Wally and I pooled our meat cubes to make a beef stew that we had with biscuits and sweet tea and I used some spare hot water to have a shave.

One of the platoons was planning to advance to hold a rise in the ground about a half a mile ahead and I suggested to Farrell that I should go along, but he was not enthusiastic, possibly because my rank was higher. Instead, he asked me to 'hold the fort' whilst he made a tour of his troops. All went well and I had no problems during my temporary command.

Repatriation

Early on D + 2, I received a message that all glider pilots were to be repatriated and I sent an order out to the platoons that No 5 Flight was to collect at Company HQ. When all except those with the furthest platoon had arrived, we set forth in open order. Our route took us through Ranville which had suffered a heavy shelling and appeared to be deserted. On either side of the road, there were yellow signs bearing the 'death head' and the warning '*minen*', and I was grateful that the Germans had not mined our landing area. Our next contact was a troop of Sherman tanks and the ribbing between our pilots going back and their crews moving forward was great value.

After a short distance we came to the bridges over the Caen Canal and the River Orne, both of which were now held by the Lovatt Scouts. There we saw the wreckage of the six gliders that had been flown in overnight, and the most remarkable achievement of two pilots who landed right on the bridge in the dark. This operation had been vital, for the crossings had to be held at all cost against the anticipated German counter-attack, and subsequently for use by the British force's advance towards Paris. After a fierce battle in which the glider pilots took part, both bridges were taken and occupied until relieved by Commando Units.

Whilst our journey back did not take us past the gun emplacements at Merville, we understood that two of the three gliders landed fairly close but had experienced the greatest difficulty in recognising the target because prior shelling by the Navy and bombing had covered the whole area with a dense cloud of dust. Furthermore, the help from the Rebecca/Eureka 'homing device' did not materialise due to a freak accident. Because the equipment was 'top secret', the parachutist carrying it had a small explosives charge in his kitbag to destroy it if necessary. Unfortunately, the plunger on the charge was out when the kitbag hit the ground and the jolt caused the explosion which blew up everything. Nevertheless the gliders landed sufficiently near for the troops carried to join the parachutists in capturing the battery, and the guns were destroyed.

After the 'Pegasus' bridge, as it was subsequently named, we approached Ouistreham, the seaside town behind Sword beach. There we were told that the defenders had put up a determined resistance and the whole place looked a complete shambles. The beach itself, when we came to it, appeared to house every type of obstacle: large 'hedgehogs' of heavy iron girders standing ten feet high, thick iron poles with mines lashed on top, jagged steel rails and huge concrete angular blocks. Behind it all there were what remained of numerous gun emplacements.

The beach clearance teams, working with bulldozers, had already established firm exit ramps and berthing areas for small vessels, but beyond those, the stretch of sand was littered with numerous wrecked landing craft of all sizes, abandoned tanks and vehicles, and every type of battle equipment.

Lined up on the beach, there was also the welcome sight of six tank-landing craft and as the pilots arrived, an officer directed them to one of these and ordered them to disperse nearby until told to board.

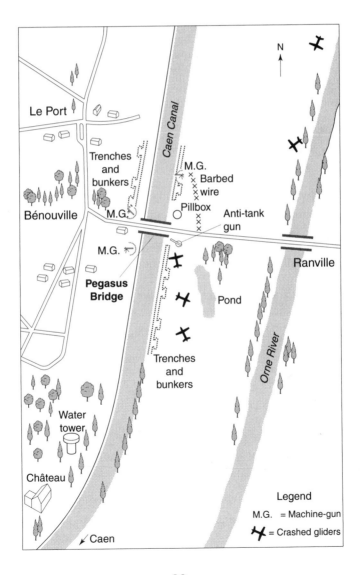

I managed to keep my Flight together and when the craft was nearly afloat, we waded out and climbed up the ramp to settle in the well of the vessel. I then made my way to the bridge and contacted the captain.

'Do you want any men to give you a push into deeper water?' I asked.

'No thanks' came the reply, 'we are practically afloat now and will be free in a few minutes. Tell your chaps to make themselves at home. Once away, we will be bringing them some hot tea and later will hand out those self-heating tins of soup which should be warming.'

'Thank you, that will be most welcome. Tell me, where are we heading and what is the sea like?'

'We dock at Littlehampton and the sea has settled considerably now the wind has dropped. We had no trouble from Jerry coming out and battleships are covering us all the way, so we should have a quiet trip. Ah, Ah, we are off the sand, so will ease back gently as there are still submerged spikes around. Will you excuse me please. I will get her underway.' With that, he assumed command and the engines started up to a cheer from the pilots as we slowly turned to the starboard and set course for England.

I then went down to the main body of the craft where the pilots had parked themselves on inflatable liferafts and were happily chatting and reliving once more, the great experience of landing in France.

Throughout the voyage, the Navy looked after us admirably and it hardly seemed long before we could see the dim outline of the Sussex coast. I must confess a wonderful feeling of gratitude to be back, safe and sound, and as we entered the little harbour and tied up alongside a stone jetty, I called for three cheers for the Navy. First on board was the Adjutant who told us that transport awaited to take us to a school where a hot meal, shower and somewhere to rest was provided. I don't know its name but it was obviously a smart girls college although it had an annoying feature of a bell that seemed to be ringing continuously, that was until I found the reason, a notice which read: 'If in need of a mistress, press the bell.'

Collecting the Stragglers

After a most welcome meal, I had a shower (soap and towel provided) and settled on a bed for a snooze, only to be awoken by the Adjutant.

'John, you're just the chap! As most of the pilots are back, I will transport them to Fargo Camp, but I would ask you to wait behind and cope with the stragglers. I will leave you a truck, so please get down to the docks and pick up any late arrivals until, let's say 8 o'clock.'

'Right. I will be happy to do that because I am missing six pilots who I know were with a distant platoon.' What I did not say was that we were only 12 miles from my home in Bognor and I could telephone Eileen, my wife, and give her the good news of my safe return.

I hung around the jetty until 8 o'clock and was just about to push off when a small landing craft arrived and there were my six, waving happily. They had obviously been on the scrounge during their way to the beach for they were festooned with mine signs, German helmets and rifles. Having returned on a small craft, however, they were hungry and as our cooks had already packed up and returned to Depot, I had to devise a plan to feed them. Happily our route back passed through Chichester and so I again telephoned Eileen and asked her to meet me at the Dolphin Hotel with as much money as she could raise.

We then embussed and drove the 15 miles to Chichester, where I went into the hotel to see the manager.

'Look,' I explained, 'I am Captain Morrison, a glider pilot. We landed in Normandy on D-Day and have just been pulled out of the front line and returned to England. There are six chaps outside, dirty and battle exhausted, who have not eaten for two days and I wonder if you would please organise food and drink for them. My wife is now driving over from Bognor with as much money as she can raise from her family, but if it is insufficient will you trust me to send you the difference?'

'Forget it Captain,' came the immediate response. 'I am proud to help. Please bring them in and it will be my honour to look after them. How about steak, bacon, eggs and chips to start off, with as much drink as they would like?'

I went outside to tell the chaps, only to find a crowd of admirers who had gathered around, eager to shake hands with their heroes. Indeed, as the pilots trooped into the hotel, complete with their 'loot', the numbers suddenly increased as the word went around, and shortly the beer tankards really stacked up!

Having seen them settled, I looked round and there was Eileen, grinning from ear to ear. 'Glad to see you back darling,' she whispered. 'Are you all right? Was it too terrible? I have scrounged eighty pounds from Father, that's all he had. Will it be enough?'

'Actually, the meal is on the house, so I won't need it after all. Thanks anyway. It is wonderful to see you Honey and if you will just give me a couple of minutes, I will arrange coffee and cakes for the driver and something for us. I will then give you the "front line" story.'

For the next hour, we chatted whilst I kept a watchful eye on the pilots who were embellishing their account with all sorts of adventures. Eventually when replete and full of beer, we thanked the hotel manager and embussed somewhat noisily. With a number of urgent stops *en route*, we finally arrived back at Fargo Camp at 1 o'clock to find it in complete darkness with everybody asleep.

No-one wanted to see me, neither could the Guard Room tell us where to sleep. So there was nothing for it but to doss down on the sofas in the Sergeant's Mess and the lads were soon snoring merrily. The following morning, complete with hangovers, the 'stragglers' were re-equipped by the Quartermaster and we joined up with the rest of the Flight to be transported back to RAF Keevil where our 'welcome home' was fabulous!

A Horsa glider on her final landing approach flies over an Armstrong Whitworth Whitley. The Whitley was designed as a bomber and saw service as such in the early years of the war. As more powerful four-engined bombers came into service, the aircraft was utilised as a glider tug for the Horsa during the later years of the conflict.

Ready for D-Day! Thirty Hamilcar gliders and two Horsas queue on the runway at Tarrant Rushton in readiness for the invasion of German-occupied Europe in 1944. Their Handley Page Halifax tow-planes are parked on either side of the runway ready to advance and connect to their charges as the runway clears. The Halifax was the only aircraft to tow the large Hamilcars. D-Day stripes are clearly visible on all the aircraft. *(Imperial War Museum; CL26)*

FIVE

AFTER D-DAY

Rest Camp

On 12 June, I was instructed to attend a meeting with the Operations Officer to give an account of my Flight's action in Normandy. As I had already made a report to my Squadron Commander, I collected my papers and duly sought out Major Andrews at Wing Headquarters.

'Welcome home John,' he greeted me, 'it's good to see you again. I've been given the job of writing about the Regiment's performance during the invasion and would like to have your story.'

'Fine Andy. Actually, I have made a report to John Lyne and have a copy of it with me. To save you time, may I suggest that you first read it and then I will be happy to fill in any further information that you may require.'

'That's great John,' he said reaching for the papers, 'give me a few minutes.' He then read through the document. After he had finished, he asked questions to obtain further detail of the flight, the landing and the reaction of my pilots under fire, and finally congratulated us on a task well undertaken.

'Now John,' he continued, 'it seems as though your chaps had a rough time out on the left flank and could do with a rest.'

'A rest?' I interrupted, 'we are fine and cannot wait to get into action with the 1st Airborne.'

'Yes, I'm sure, but that phase has been put back by Monty. Caen has proved to be a tougher nut than was originally anticipated, and it seems that he is not prepared to move until larger forces are available. In the meantime, the Colonel would like you to take your pilots to a 'rest camp' that has been set up at Watchet, which is near Minehead.'

'But we don't need a rest,' I protested, 'and the chaps are now all raring to get back into the fight.'

'You will do as you are told,' chortled Andy, putting his arm round my shoulders, 'and I promise that I will give you plenty of notice before the next operation. Now buzz off for two weeks and enjoy yourselves.'

Thus, for the remainder of June, my flight 'rested' in a tented camp located on top of some low cliffs, right by the sea. The weather was perfect and strangely enough, my only worry was that the pilots might become bored.

Fortunately, one of my officers, Lt Ken Chittleburgher, was a champion swimmer and he took over the learners and also trained a swimming team at the municipal baths so that we could challenge the locals during their next gala. At this enjoyable function which, thanks to Ken, we won easily, four of the chaps gave a 'ditching demonstration' off the top diving board and someone carefully left the inflated dinghy with a few coins in it by the exit. Luckily, the citizens of Minehead took the hint and the Flight went home with some spending money.

After a while I thought that we should have a change and, having looked around, I discovered that we were right on the edge of Exmoor where there was an artillery field firing range that was not being used. This was perfect for my ideas on further training. All my pilots had experience under fire, now I wanted them to practise as a fighting unit, using live ammunition. Having cleared it with the authorities, we took off to march, each with full kit and an airborne sleeping bag to the Moor where Lt Bill Sykes had found a delightful spot located beside a freshwater stream. For the next week we lived out in the open and spent our days advancing over beautiful country, pooping off at pre-planned targets. Without doubt, all of us became more efficient and gained confidence.

Operation *Falaise* Trap

Our return to RAF Keevil was followed by a couple of 'false starts' when we were told to stand-to and await a briefing, but in each case the plan was dropped. Then, at the end of July, the longed-for breakthrough took place when the American forces, with a massive air support of heavy bombers, cut through the Wehrmacht's defensive crust and fanned out behind the Germans. At the same time the British and Canadians bypassed Caen and advanced southwards.

Hitler's reaction was to order his armoured divisions to counterattack towards the beaches, which strategy, according to his commanders, was fraught with danger and so it proved, for the German plan failed and the armour and supporting infantry were stranded when the Allied forces started to close in. General Patton swung his advance to meet up with the Canadian First Army at Falaise to trap the German Divisions, whilst the retreating tanks and transports were mercilessly destroyed by rocket-firing fighters.

A total of 12,000 German troops were killed and 50,000 captured. That is when the planners decided 'to put the cork in the bottle' and completely seal the trap by sending in a squadron of Special Air Service to harass the units that were slipping out. They were to fly in immediately by glider and it was decided that 'John Morrison is just the chap for the job!'

The SAS pitched up on the afternoon of 17 August in their jeeps which had heavy machine-guns mounted to fire over the driver's head. The sides and floor were heavily armoured and each jeep and trailer was fully packed with mines and ammunition. To me it looked a pretty heavy load and, in order to establish where they were to be locked into the glider, I arranged for them to be weighed. It was just as well because they were 50% over our limit.

'No problem,' was the happy response from Captain James Bates, their CO. 'We will strip off all armour.'

This brought the weight down to 4 tons which was still overloaded but as there was little else that they could do to reduce further, I approached our tug skip. 'Davie,' I said 'tomorrow as you know, I am delivering an SAS Squadron into France but their load consists of a jeep with machine-gun and trailer packed solid with mines. They have already stripped off the armour round the jeep but I am still nearly a ton overweight. I have never piloted an extra heavy glider before, and quite honestly, I don't know what to expect, but I am prepared to have a go provided you are happy to tow us.'

'Oh John,' came the reply, 'I am sure that the Stirling will be powerful enough. I think it will be a case of using plenty of runway, because once we are up, there should not be any trouble. Tell you what. There is one way of finding out, let's try a dummy run and you can always drop the tow if you feel that we are not going to make it. It is still daylight, so load up and I will organise the flight and ground crew for 6 o'clock.'

I immediately contacted Bates and told him of the plan and it was not long before he met me at my glider and manhandled the jeep and trailer on board to their correct station where they were firmly secured. Fortunately, we had the longest runway and our tug wasted no time in pulling away. To be on the safe side, I held the glider down until we had built up speed and then eased the controls back. We came off all right but dear me, my aircraft seemed to be wallowing all over the place and was slow to respond. However, the tug was now accelerating, although Davie also seemed to be leaving the lift-off until the last moment. Much to my relief, the Stirling rose to climb steadily and I followed.

'That was all right wasn't it No 7? How is it at your end of the rope?'

'Not too bad No 1,' I replied, 'but it is like flying a barge, the controls are so heavy.'

'Yes, we can feel the drag, but it should improve as we gather speed.

I suggest that we take you round at 1500 feet and you can drop the tow when you feel like it.'

Accordingly, on the crosswind leg, I turned to my second pilot, Wally Beech. 'I think that I will allow plenty of height in our approach, Wally. Pull the tow-release now and bring down half flap but hold "full" until I give you the nod.'

It was just as well that I was cautious, because as we flew towards the runway, I suddenly realised that we were dropping like a stone! I had already committed us to half-flap and it was thus a case of extending our glide to the maximum. So, holding breath, I kept speed just above stalling and, by the smallest of margins scraped over the airfield fence to 'dump' down short of the tarmac. The SAS Captain was not too impressed!

However, the exercise had its value because I was able to warn my pilots about what to expect. That evening we had a session with the SAS who handed out maps. The latest information was that the American Third Army under Patton had advanced rapidly east towards Paris and XX Corps took Chartres on 16 August. In effect this sealed further German retreat to the south, but the area around the trap at Falaise still held some of their Army Group 'B'. Accordingly, the plan was to land the SAS who would have the task of sorting out any escaping transport. At 0800 hrs on the morning of 18 August, I briefed the Flight.

By virtue of the fact that this was a comparatively small operation, there was no laid out landing strip but we were given an area that we were to use and, after landing, it was up to the individual jeeps to make their way to the Squadron RV. Thereafter, as there was no space for the glider pilots on the vehicles, we were to set up a fighting unit to assist and ultimately to join up with the Canadian First Army.

After checking weapons, the Section Officers took over and organised loading of their gliders and at 1100 hrs Operation *Falaise* started. I have not given details of the take-off because we were hardly airborne when Davie came on the 'intercom'.

'Hello No 7, I have news for you. The operation has been cancelled and we are to return to base.'

'Bloody Hell Skipper. What's going on? . . . Why?'

'I don't know. Just "return to base" so I am turning back now.'

Leaving Wally to fly the glider, I made my way to Capt. Bates and gave him the news. For minutes he swore continuously and I must confess that I joined in with the rest of his crew. This time I allowed plenty of height and we landed safely at speed. We had hardly come to a halt when a jeep roared up and an SAS Colonel jumped out.

'James,' he shouted, 'thank God I stopped you. Apparently the Canadians reckon that they have all the Jerries in the bag and have cancelled your trip. Don't worry, I guess that the powers are saving us for Paris!'

Only four gliders took off and, whilst we were all disappointed, I always had the feeling that, as far as we were concerned, our Flight's plan for action once we had landed was a bit woolly! To cheer up Bates, I took him and his officers back to the Mess for a couple of beers before lunch and when leaving, he presented me with an American Airborne repeater rifle which I treasured.

Following the cancellation of Operation *Falaise*, it was abundantly clear that Monty had the Germans on the run. Paris was occupied on 25 August and, during September, the British XXX Corps advanced rapidly through Belgium. The 1st Airborne Division was still not being used and from rumours filtering down, the Parachute Regiments were hankering to get into the battle once more. Indeed we were all on tenterhooks for I was convinced that something big was in the offing. I didn't have long to wait.

Six

OPERATION *MARKET GARDEN* – ARNHEM

Standby

Saturday 16 September 1944
The morning dawned dull and overcast, with the prospect of yet another dreary day of drizzle that, over the past week, had transformed the lovely Lincolnshire countryside into a murky haze through which the woods stood out like dark shadows. Pulling aside the blackout curtains, I glowered at the leaden clouds and groaned in apprehension at the task of stimulating, once more, the enthusiasm of my pilots who had already spent ten weary days in a state of static standby.

My concern stemmed from the fact that, for sometime now, the men had been maintained to peak battle readiness. They were supremely fit, mentally and physically tough and 'rarin' to get stuck in' and, having been transferred with their gliders to an aerodrome on the east coast of England, were anticipating early action. But, like so many false starts in the past, it was beginning to look like yet another damp squib. Even so, somehow, I had to find ways and means of keeping them mean-ingfully occupied and, to this end, had called a meeting with my Flight Officers immediately after breakfast.

Whilst walking back to our quarters, my thoughts were suddenly shattered by the harsh metallic sound of the Tannoy.

'Airborne "O" Group will report to the Briefing Centre immediately, I repeat, Airborne "O" Group will report to the Briefing Centre immediately.'

'Thank goodness,' I thought, 'maybe at long last this is it,' and promptly broke into a trot towards my room where I buckled on my revolver and grabbed my map-case. Fortunately, my second-in-command, Lt Bill Sykes, had already anticipated my departure for briefing and I turned to find him standing in the doorway with a grin on his face from ear to ear. 'OK Skipper,' he said, 'I will organise a weapons check and have the chaps ready for your return.'

'Thanks Bill, let's hope we will take off this time.' Turning on my heel, I made my way smartly to the long Nissen hut which served as a Briefing Centre.

As I approached the entrance, I was conscious that there was already a short queue of officers from the various Airborne Companies being subjected to close scrutiny by two Provost Sergeants sitting at a table, who checked each name against a typed list. Soon it was my turn.

'Capt. J. Morrison, Officer Commanding No 5 Flight Glider Pilot Regiment,' I announced to a florid-looking soldier who glanced down at his papers and having found my name, handed me some Roneod sheets and a map.

Moving towards the door, I paused for a brief moment to take in the sight of a room brightly illuminated with lines of fluorescent lamps. I suppose the room was about 150 ft long by 60 ft wide, with a low plat-form across the whole of the far end. The back wall was covered with maps upon which coloured tapes indicated the assault routes. The side windows were already covered with blackout curtains and, stretching from front to back were twenty rows of trestle tables with chairs, partly occupied by groups of officers poring over maps. All around, looking grimly expectant, were some of the commanders of the seasoned Parachute and Air Landing Battalions of the 1st Airborne Division, who had seen action in North Africa and Sicily and who, for 14 months had been anxiously awaiting the opportunity to have another go at the Hun.

Seeing one of the Glider Pilot Flight Commanders sitting near the front, I made my way over to him.

'Hullo John,' he exclaimed, waving his printed orders, 'I see you will be flying in the 1st Anti-tank Guns. Well the best of luck! I've got a company of South Staffs, in fact, our Squadron will be flying in the regiment. A piece of cake!' His 'good wishes' were obviously prompted by the fact that, in action, it is far easier to unload a glider carrying soldiers with hand weapons than a jeep, trailer and 6-pound anti-tank gun.

'Hold on old chap,' I protested, 'let me sit down first. Now, where are we going?'

'Arnhem, of course!'

I suppose that I should have guessed, because only seven days pre-viously, I had attended a similar briefing for Operation *Comet*, in which it had been planned to capture the three main bridges over the Maas, Waal and Rhine Rivers with only the 1st Airborne Division and the Polish Brigade. Now, obviously, the planners had recognised the extent of this task and having cancelled Operation *Comet*, had re-constructed the assault using a far larger force under the code-name *Market Garden*.

In retrospect, I often wonder if the news of the original plan might not have reached the ears of German Intelligence. After all, it only required a chance remark to a WAAF waitress in the Mess such as, 'We should have been in Arnhem today' and the damage would have been done. War historians have subsequently discounted that prior knowledge had been acquired by the Germans, but I am sure that many on the 'receiving end' will still have their doubts as to the security of the operation.

However, that did not concern me then and I had just started to read the Operation Order when we were called to attention by the arrival of a group of Staff Officers headed by the GI who promptly jumped onto the low platform and stood for a few seconds, surveying the assembly.

'OK chaps . . . settle down. First I will give you the general plan of *Market Garden*, then Brigadier Intelligence will provide details of the German dispositions as we know them and, finally, I will run through the Operation Order for the 1st Airborne Division and in particular, the battle objectives of the units here.'

In anticipation, we sat there with bated breath to hear the master strategy in which we were to be a major factor in bringing about victory in Northern Europe and we were not disappointed. As the plan unfolded, so we realised the enormity of the operation.

Briefing

Grasping a pointer the GI revealed the general plan:

> 'As you will know, XXX Corps, under the command of General Horrocks, has made great progress and are now regrouping just short of the Belgian–Dutch border. The master plan, under the code name *Market Garden* is designed to spearhead an assault by land forces northwards through Holland round the top of the German fortifications, and to drive on to Berlin from the north-west.
>
> 'The first phase is for the Guards Armoured Division to make a 65-mile dash to Arnhem and to enable them to achieve this, three Airborne divisions will first be dropped to capture and hold all the vital bridges and canal crossings *en route*, thereby providing a carpet over which XXX Corps will advance.
>
> 'In greater detail, Major-General Maxwell Taylor's American 101st Airborne Division will capture the river and canal crossings between Eindhoven and Veghel. North of them, Brigadier-General James Garvin's 82nd Airborne Division will take and hold the area between Grave and Nijmegen, which includes the Maas and Waal River bridges. Finally, probably the most important objective, Arnhem, with its 400-yard long bridge over the Lower Rhine will be secured and held

by the 1st British Airborne Division, together with the 1st Polish Parachute Brigade.

'In all, 35,000 men together with equipment, jeeps and guns are to be lifted by transport aircraft and some 2500 gliders from no less than 24 airfields. This is a formidable task which, due to limitations on the availability of suitable aircraft, will have to be carried out in three "lifts" on successive days. Right, so much for the general plan, now Brigadier Johnson will brief you on the opposition that you may expect.'

A tall, dapper-looking officer then moved to the centre of the platform and gave a brief summary of the known troops in northern Holland which, incidentally, made no reference to the two depleted divisions of German armour in the Arnhem area!

Finally, the GI resumed the briefing with a run down of the objectives of the 1st Airborne Division.

'On 17 September, the 1st Parachute Brigade will drop onto DZ "Z" [Drop Zone "Z"], eight miles from Arnhem, with orders to seize the main road bridge and also the pontoon bridge. At the same time, the 1st Airlanding Brigade, carried in 345 Horsa and 13 Hamilcar gliders to LZ "Z" [Landing Zone "Z"], will first secure the landing zones for the next day and then occupy the north and south banks of the Rhine.

'On Monday 18 September, the 4th Parachute Brigade will drop onto DZ "Y" to occupy the high ground north of Arnhem, whilst on LZ "S" the remainder of the 1st Airlanding Brigade with the Royal Artillery and other supporting troops will be flown in by 287 Horsa and 15 Hamilcar gliders.

'Finally, on Thursday 19 September, the 1st Polish Independent Parachute Brigade will drop onto DZ "K", 2 miles south of the bridge, with orders to secure the approaches from the south. This day will also be used for the resupply of food and ammunition. Such is the overall plan. Further detail will be found in the documents issued to you. I wish you all good luck.'

Instructions to Glider Pilots were that we should fight with the units that we had carried until the Divisional Sector had been established and then assemble as a Regiment in the area of Sonsbeek (743785) which was 2 miles north of the main Arnhem bridge. Although not mentioned, the orders for my Flight were slightly different in that we were to fly in the 1st Airborne Anti-tank Battery on 18 September, but, because they already had the full gun crews crowded onto their jeeps and it would not be possible to travel with them, my pilots would fight as an independent unit until released by Brigade to proceed to Sonsbeek.

The briefing completed, I made my way across the hut to contact Major Bill Arnold, Officer Commanding the Anti-tank Battery and arranged to meet him later to discuss the loading problems and to allocate gliders so that the pilots and gunners could get to know each other. Then, complete with map and notes, I made my way back to the Flight hut to brief my pilots on their battle orders. As I entered, I noticed that the men were lined up in the three sections with their respective officers, Bill Sykes, Ken Chittleburgher and Roy Martin at the head.

Apart from the officers, in the Glider Pilot Regiment the First Pilot holds the rank of a Staff Sergeant, whilst his assistant or Second Pilot is usually a Sergeant. It followed therefore that as Commander, I briefed the Flight as a whole and not just the Section Officers, as would be the case in a normal army O Group.

'Well chaps, this looks like the real thing! It's Arnhem again, but this time with a full Division.' I then went on to repeat the known information about the German troops, the overall strategy, our own Flight's orders and finished by instructing the Section Officers to check the glider crews, the weapons and ammunition.

'This afternoon the Flight will parade at 1400 hrs and will march down to the Anti-tank Battery who are in tents over yonder to meet up with the gun crews you will be carrying. It is understandable that they will be apprehensive, so make friends and cut out "line shooting". We will start loading tomorrow immediately after the first wave has left, so use any spare time that you have to sort yourselves out and write letters home. Leave the envelopes open as all letters will be censored.'

Start of *Market Garden*

Sunday 17 September
So it was that at 1030 hrs on a bright Sunday morning, we stood at the side of the runway to watch and cheer as the first wave of aircraft carrying parachutists took off. They certainly went with our good wishes and fervent prayers for we all realised that our lives depended on their ability to secure safe landing zones for us because, on the second day, there would certainly be no element of surprise.

At last the final 'Dak' roared away to leave the airstrip still and silent with groups of pilots and ground crews lost in their private thoughts, but not for long because we then had to set about loading our own gliders. To do this, the jeeps and guns had to be driven up a ramp to the side door of the Horsa and then manhandled to swing round 90° to their allocated places, facing the tail. It was a back-breaking job involving considerable physical effort but, after thirty minutes or so, I was satisfied that all equipment was on board, secured firmly with quick-release strainers and locked into the correct stations. Leaving my Second Pilot, Sergeant Parker, to tidy up, I went round to check personally that every glider in my Flight was loaded correctly and ready to take off.

The pilots then spent the rest of the morning 'personalising' their gliders with slogans. On my glider, one of the Staff Sergeants had kindly drawn the Flight badge just below the cockpit. It consisted of a Roman numeral five with wings sprouting from the right leg of the V and, in action, would serve the purpose of indicating where I had landed.

After a quick lunch, we were all back at the runway and it was not long before, in the distance, we could discern the first of the returning aircraft. I must confess that it was exhilarating to see the good old Dakotas lined up to the distant horizon, one behind the other, roaring steadily towards the runway with wheels down to land in quick succession. We all stood, waving them on and, when they passed, we could recognise the pilots responding to our welcome with a thumbs-up sign.

As the aircraft taxied slowly round the perimeter track to their dispersal points, I ran over to find my own tug pilot to hear his news, but apart from a few shouted comments before they boarded their transport, I had to be satisfied with the knowledge that they had had a successful flight.

Subsequently, I sat down with the crews whilst they had a late lunch to hear of their experiences over Holland. The general feeling about the flight route to Arnhem was that there had been a few unpleasant moments crossing the coast when the German anti-aircraft guns had opened fire, but that these had been attacked immediately by rocket-firing Typhoons who neutralised them. The approach to Arnhem itself had been reasonably quiet and the drop successful. As far as they could see, there had been little resistance on the Dropping Zone itself except perhaps the odd burst of machine-gun fire.

'What do you think of our prospects tomorrow?' I asked.

'Well there is no doubt that the first wave had the benefit of surprise and I rather think that it will depend on whether the airborne chaps can get through to the bridge and hold the approaches to it. Jerry will then have to concentrate on them and with luck, the future Landing Zones, some ten miles away, will be reasonably clear.'

Understandably, we were all elated with the news and the occasion could have developed into a celebration with the RAF crews. However, good sense prevailed and, after a couple of beers with my officers, I decided to make an early night of it. So, having checked my gear, automatic rifle, ammunition and grenades, I turned in to sleep soundly until early call on the next day.

Monday 18 September
By 0500hrs I was up, showered, shaved and feeling genuinely excited. On looking outside, however, I realised that the aerodrome was enveloped in a ground mist. 'Never mind, it will clear with the sun,' I thought and with a light heart walked over to the Flight hut to check if the lads were up. I needn't have worried for, from the building came the chorus of our Flight song to the tune of 'Pistol packing Mama' led by the inimitable Staff Sergeant Gibbons:

> Lay that baby down boys,
> Lay that glider down,
> Glider pranging 5 Flight,
> Lay her gently down.

Standing in the mist outside the door, I felt proud of those fine men. They had tremendous loyalty both for the Flight and for each other and certainly must have been one of the best units in the Regiment. My entry was greeted with happy comments such as 'The show must be on chaps, even the Boss is up'. All was well, so I pushed off to breakfast.

Arnhem: 17 September 1944. These four Horsa gliders have recently landed and are in the process of disgorging men and equipment before one of the hardest-fought battles of World War II. *(Imperial War Museum; CL1174)*

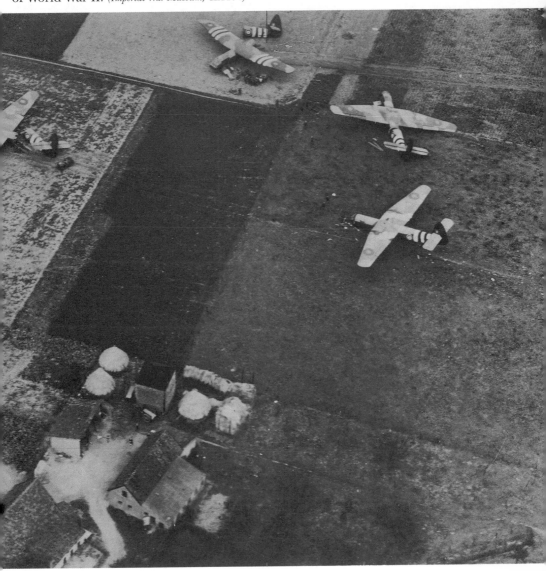

A Tetrarch tank claws its way from the cavernous fuselage of a Hamilcar glider. These enormous aircraft had a wingspan of 110 feet and could carry either one tank or forty troops. During the Arnhem operation, the British airborne forces had 812 Horsas and 64 Hamilcars at their disposal. *(Imperial War Museum; TP4345F)*

Seven

Into Battle

Take-off

As the earlier MET reports were confident that the ground mist would lift, we originally planned to be away by 0900 hrs. However, this was not to be. After sitting in our glider on the towpath for an hour, I received the message that take-off would be put back until midday. At the time, little did we know that this delay, though frustrating to the extreme, would be a heaven-sent blessing in disguise. By a quirk of fate, a document setting out the whole 'Top Secret' *Market Garden* plan was discovered by the Germans on the body of a dead American whose glider had been shot down. It was in the hands of Colonel General Kurt Student on the evening of the first day and full details setting out the times of the successive lifts, the landing and dropping zones and even the routes to be followed by the aircraft, were transmitted to Field Marshal Walter Model at his Arnhem Headquarters overnight!

As a result, early the next morning, 190 German fighters were airborne awaiting the arrival of the Allied Armada. By 11.00 a.m., however, as there was no sign of tugs and gliders, it was assumed by the *Luftwaffe* that the information was a diversionary fake and half the aircraft were ordered back to their bases whilst the remainder patrolled the skies over northern Holland. Thus, when we in the second wave finally arrived, most of the German squadrons were in the wrong sector or were being refuelled. What a let off!

After a cup of 'char', I was back at the towpath where the huge Horsas were lined up just short of an intersection. As I was the leading glider, the tow rope was already attached to the wings of my aircraft so that when my Dakota tug taxied onto the runway and had straightened up, all the ground crew had to do was to connect the intercom plug at the other end into its tail socket.

Before climbing aboard, I strolled down the long line of gliders to give a final word of encouragement to my pilots. As there appeared to be no problems, I made my way back to 'V5' and, having checked that the Second Pilot and the gun crew were happily settled, closed and secured the side door.

During this time the aerodrome had become a hive of activity with Dakotas taking off on a separate runway with the parachute boys. Sitting quietly in our Perspex cockpit, it seemed an age before our own departure was due, but then, right on the dot, a long line of Daks was to be seen moving up the perimeter track to the lead-in strip. Our own tug then turned onto the towpath approximately 80 yards in front of my glider, and was quickly hooked to the tow-rope and the intercom connected.

'Hello Matchbox,' called the pilot, 'how are you feeling?'

'Great Skipper and raring to go.'

'Well I guess we had better get moving.'

He slowly took up the slack and, upon the green light from the ground controller, opened up the throttles so that we started to roll forward in a cloud of dust. Gradually, the combination gathered speed and out of the corner of my eye I could see various cars and trucks on the side of the runway with the occupants waving us off. As we accelerated over the joints of the tarmac, the sound of the wheels became louder and louder . . . *clunk* . . . *te clunk* . . . *te clunk* . . . rather like a train, until I was able to ease back on the control column and my heavily ladened aircraft literally staggered into the air. Holding her just ten feet above the runway, we flew still faster until finally the tug took off to gain height and turn onto the first leg of our journey to the assembly point at Aldeburgh.

'OK Matchbox,' came the cheery call, 'we seemed to manage that all right. I suppose the next problem is to find our way.'

'Don't worry No 1, Parkie here has a map, so your navigator can take a kip.'

'Thanks Buddy,' came a Canadian drawl, 'after last night, I guess I can do with it.'

At the assembly point we were joined by streams of other transports which were to take the northern route and, in all, flying practically wingtip to wingtip, was a total of 1336 C-47 Dakotas and 340 Stirlings, together with 1205 gliders. We formed a massive air armada over 100 miles long!

There were planes everywhere and I was beginning to ponder if there was enough air space for us all when my reverie was suddenly shattered by the first of many vicious sideslips that were quite terrifying. What had happened was that the slipstream from one of the huge bomber aircraft ahead had created a tremendous air turbulence which had hit only one wing of my glider, forcing it to swing away and to drop drastically. This, in turn, yanked the tail of the tug sideways and down and, if we had not succeeded in bringing our aircraft back onto station by heaving on the column, the whole combination would have been out of control.

Whilst we had been aware of this problem from previous operations, the numbers of aircraft were now far greater than before and this presented a constant hazard which gave pilots a terrible strain of anticipation. Sadly, in the whole *Market Garden* operation, a total of 58 British and American pilots failed to reach their destination, either because the tow-rope had parted or the tug had been forced to unhook.

By now we had left the English coast far behind. It had become slightly cloudy, yet I could clearly see the white crests of the choppy sea below with the occasional rescue boat following our course. Way above, there wheeled a continuous cover of fighter aircraft on whom our safety depended.

After what seemed to be only a few minutes, my Second Pilot called out 'coast ahead' and there we were passing over the yellow sand dunes of Holland. Our route took us past Schouwen Island where areas of the coastal belt had been flooded by the Germans and everywhere was looking so peaceful, when suddenly, five miles ahead, all hell broke loose. German anti-aircraft guns both on the ground and in flak-ships had opened up on the leading aircraft carrying the parachute companies and within seconds they were completely engulfed by angry black puffs.

'Now we are for it Parkie,' I shouted, 'it looks as though we will just have to fly through that lot, so keep your fingers crossed.' Luckily, our guardian angels in the form of dozens of Typhoon fighters were onto them in a trice. They tore into those German guns with their rockets and murderous machine-gun fire and by the time we were over the danger zone, they had all been silenced.

'Well,' I said, 'it seems we are in luck today, so earn your pay and show me where we are on the map.' Actually, throughout the flight, we had been able to listen into the conversations of the tug crew and follow the position reports of the navigator who shortly was to record our crossing the Maas and then the Waal rivers.

'Get ready Matchbox,' came the call, 'the Rhine is 20 miles ahead.'

'OK Skipper, I can see it now. That's the bridge way over to the starboard. I'll be casting off soon. Thanks for the tow.'

'Good luck chaps, see you shortly.'

We approached our Landing Zone at about 1800 feet, and could see the coloured parachutes of the 1st Brigade dotted around the DZs 'X' and 'Z', whilst the previous wave of gliders, noticeable from their 'run-up' tracks, seemed to litter the landscape like stranded whales. At last I could discern our own field ahead, which had been marked with coloured smoke by the Independent Parachute Company and, when we were ready, my Second Pilot pulled the lever which released the glider. With a crack, the tow parted and our tug, with the rope whipping below, turned away to port for its return journey. We continued to fly quite fast until I eased back on the column to reduce speed prior to applying the large flaps in the 'half down' position.

It was then we were aware that the constant noise and rattle of the tow had faded and for a brief moment we could enjoy the silence of free flight before concentrating on the urgent task of landing quickly in the correct area. When the speed had dropped sufficiently, I called for 'full flap' and, as the glider responded, I pushed forward hard on the control column, as far as it would go, until the nose was pointing straight down to just short of the near side boundary of our LZ. 'V5' literally dropped out of the sky and, as with the barn door-type flaps the speed remains constant, I experienced the peculiar sensation of the ground appearing to come right up to me.

At 100 feet, I levelled out and then holding her just above the heath, we skimmed towards the far hedge. Eventually the two main wheels connected and, with a roaring noise, we ploughed through the heather in a cloud of dust to run right up to our station where, with a touch on the brakes, we skidded to a standstill. For a moment we sat in complete silence, realising that we were down safely with a perfect landing to the furthest extent of our LZ.

Then I noticed Parkie beaming happily, whilst Bill Arnold had come through to the cockpit to lead his very relieved gun crew in 'three cheers for the pilot'. However, our jubilation was short lived with the realisation that someone was taking pot shots at the glider, but fortunately, the fire was very spasmodic and, apart from the discomfort of seemingly being a 'sitting duck', it had the considerable benefit of getting everyone cracking onto the task of unloading.

As often happens in moments of crisis, we hit a problem. In theory, after landing, the pilots simply undo the holding bolts of the tail assembly which falls to the ground. The gun crew then locate a trestle under the tail end of the glider, attach two steel ramps and drive off the jeep and gun. On this occasion, our tail assembly seemed to be locked permanently into position. Obviously, some conscientious 'erk' of the ground crew had been determined that the eight securing bolts would never come loose in flight and Parkie and I, armed with ratchet spanners, threw ourselves at those wretched nuts which just would not budge.

Luckily, the jeep driver came to our aid with a tyre lever and, after much sweating and swearing, we finally unscrewed the last two when, with a mighty crash, the tail dropped to the ground. Hurriedly the gun crew heaved it to one side whilst the driver unlocked the shackles holding the jeep and gun. Then, having located the two steel ramps to bridge the gap between the now open tail and the ground, he drove the unit down to 'Mother Earth'.

Bill Arnold having quickly checked that they were ready for action, jumped aboard and with a shouted 'Thanks for the ride chaps – see you at the bridge' roared off to their Battery assembly point leaving two exhausted pilots standing beside the wreck of their faithful 'steed'. Placing my rucksack in the ditch beside the hedge, I was then able to check how the rest of the Flight were faring and my first impression was that the chaps had done a damn fine job in landing their gliders to finish up at the top end of the LZ. Unfortunately, my satisfaction was short-lived, for I noticed that one of the late-comers had over-estimated

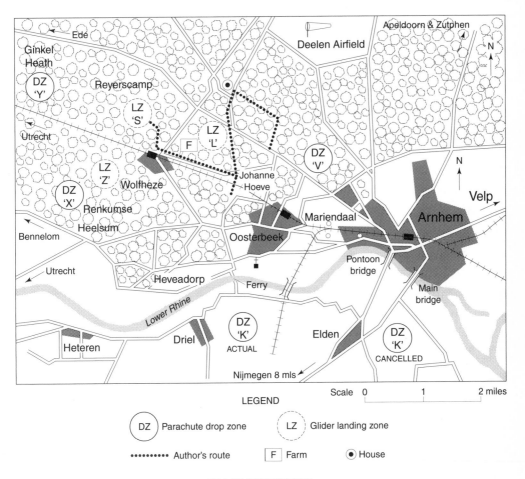

LEGEND

Scale 0 — 1 — 2 miles

DZ	Parachute drop zone	LZ	Glider landing zone
•••••••• Author's route		F Farm	⊙ House

LZ & DZ ASSIGNMENTS

LZ 'Z' = 1st (Air Landing) Brigade   DZ 'X' = 1st Parachute Brigade

LZ 'S' = 1st (Air Landing) Brigade & R.A.   DZ 'Y' = 4th Parachute Brigade

LZ 'L' = Re-supply zone   DZ 'K' = 1st Polish Independent Parachute Brigade

DZ 'V' = Re-supply zone

his height and at one stage looked as if he would not clear the front hedge. Luckily, he just made it but only reached a third of the way towards what should have been his final position.

'Blast him' I shouted, 'now we will have trouble.' Sure enough, the following Glider Pilot, having already committed himself, had to swing to the right to avoid the 'shortie' and in doing so, sideswiped the wing of another aircraft, injuring two men. From then onwards, it was a case of the remaining pilots taking avoiding action but, thank goodness, apart from some dicey landings, there were no further accidents.

I suppose that after the strain and anxiety of the journey, it was understandable that I should feel an anticlimax and, for a brief moment, I stood lethargically watching the late arrivals. Then, realising the threat of a possible attack, I set about organising an initial defensive position which was soon occupied as the pilots of 5 Flight reported in. In due course the Flight Warrant Officer, having taken count, announced, 'All present sir, except for one glider – Staff Sergeant Graham.'

Into Action

So it was in strength that we advanced in battle order on our assault route towards Arnhem. Our track led us past quite a large farm at Reijers Camp where, standing by the corner of a barn, we saw a group of Dutch civilians who waved, shouting 'Good luck'. They were all overjoyed at the prospect of victory and little did we then realise that their dreams of freedom were to take a further seven months to materialise! At the time, the possibility of failure had never entered my mind and I shared their elation by waving back at the children who were jumping up and down in their excitement.

Fortunately, the German snipers who had 'greeted' our landing must have retired because our advance was unmolested although, some 12 miles away in Arnhem, there were sounds of battle. This comparative calm enabled us to make steady progress towards the railway line and past the landing zones of the previous day where, admittedly, there were signs of skirmishes in the form of burnt out gliders and jeeps and the bodies of German and British soldiers. There seemed to be gliders everywhere. Some were standing with their wings completely severed, others were lolling on their sides with collapsed undercarriage, whilst one Hamilcar was roosting like a huge bird on top of a tree. Even so, despite the signs of wreckage strewn about, my first impressions were that the losses in men and matériel upon landing would have been minimal.

The track that we followed took a firmer surface and led past a cluster of small houses which were close to the railway line. Here again the occupants stood at their front gates, laughing and smiling. Many were wearing orange arm bands as an insignia of loyalty to their Queen. One thoughtful housewife and her husband, had stripped their apple trees and were happily handing out the contents of a cardboard box to our leading section.

By this time, quite a large column of marching troops and jeeps were converging on Wolfheze Station where the road to Oosterbeek crosses the railway line, and it was here that I was first really aware of the battle that lay ahead of us. Arnhem itself was hidden in a cloud of black smoke and although we were still eight miles away, I could distinctly hear the crump of mortar bombs and the *rat . . . tat . . . tat* of machine-guns. This was certainly not going to be a walk-over.

Our leading section had just reached the area of Wolfheze Station, when we came up to the rear company of the King's Own Scottish Border Regiment who told us that there had been resistance to their advance along the north of the railway line and that their forward company had come under heavy fire from some woods on high ground ahead. I therefore called for Lt Ken Chittleburgher, one of my officers, who rushed up from the rear section, bristling with anticipation.

'Ken,' I said, 'take it quietly. Go forward to the KOSB Battalion Headquarters and report that we have 30 Glider Pilots as a fighting unit at present with their rear company. Ask if we can help and whilst you are about it, see if you can gather information about the battle.'

'Will do Captain,' he replied, and turning on his heel he shot off at the double accompanied by his second pilot.

I smiled to myself at the thought that, he of all people, would get us into action quickly, for Ken, who was no more than five-foot tall, was one of the 'gutsiest' little guys I knew. Apart from being a champion swimmer and superbly fit, he was ever prepared to take on anything or anyone and was tremendously popular with all the Flight.

As our forward progress was now halted, I took the opportunity of tactically positioning the Sections and whilst doing so, chatted with the chaps. Like myself, they had all experienced a turbulent flight, but had 'delivered the goods' safely. No-one could tell me what had happened to the missing glider and I only hoped that they had been able to land in Allied territory.

I had hardly returned to Flight HQ when Ken puffed in and reported:

'Sir, I spoke directly to the Colonel. The news is that some of our chaps have got through to the bridge, but the general advance of the Division is meeting stiff resistance. Something is wrong with the wireless network and news is very scrappy, so the CO has sent his Intelligence Officer forward in a jeep and hopes to obtain a clearer picture soon. It also seems that some German troops are astride the wooded hill ahead of us and the advance has come under fire. They are going to sort it out. In the meantime, he asks us to remain in reserve but to send up some men to guard a dozen German prisoners until the Provost arrive.'

'OK Ken, thanks a lot. Will you please arrange for four men from your Section to find somewhere safe to locate them . . . Look, there is a tennis court in that house over there which should suit.'

By then, it was getting dusk and so, having ensured that the dejected bunch of Jerry soldiers were safely locked in, we were able to set up our own defensive position in some railway huts, where, after a brew up, we took turns to doze for a short while.

Tuesday 19 September
Before dawn the following morning, I went forward, passing through the crouching forms of Airborne soldiers on either side of the track until I found the Battalion Commanding Officer.

'Captain Morrison reporting sir. I have thirty Glider Pilots in reserve and twelve Jerries locked away in a tennis court. We are all ready to have a go.'

'OK thanks Captain, I will probably need you later. Right now my leading companies are about to assault German positions on the edge of a wood about 600 yards ahead, so if you will excuse me?'

He had hardly finished speaking when concentrated bursts of Bren-gun fire heralded the start of the attack. Realising his concern, I stepped away from his immediate circle of officers and listened to the sporadic fire and crump of grenades used to rout out the opposition. Initially the sound of the attack was continuous, but it slowly reduced in volume and, after twenty minutes or so, all that could be heard was the occasional burst of fire.

'Looks promising,' called out the elated Colonel and indeed it proved so, because within a short while a runner appeared bearing the news that the wood had been captured and the Germans had scattered, leaving behind a heavy machine-gun.

Turning to his Second-in-Command, the Colonel said, 'I am going forward to assess the position. Locate headquarters in those farm buildings over there.' Then catching sight of me, he grinned. 'Also arrange for the Glider Pilots to take over defence of the west flank.'

Pleased with the prospect of being involved, I quickly made my way back to the Flight and instructed Bill Sykes, my 2 i/c, to move the men to the area of the farm whilst I and the Section Officers made a quick recce. Fortunately the buildings were located on the corner of the wood and looked out across open meadows on three sides. There-fore a good all-round field of fire could be obtained by siting the three

Sections just inside the cover of the trees with myself alongside the centre one.

Learning from our previous experience, the pilots promptly set about digging individual foxholes and how wise the decision, for I had just sunk mine to a depth of about two feet when, suddenly without warning, all hell broke loose and the whole area was strafed continuously by German fighters.

There must have been fifteen Fw 190s which, one after the other, wheeled below the cloud and, with guns blazing, dived straight at the area where the BHQ and we were located. Shallow as it was, I dived into my foxhole with my head buried in the loose sand. Then, gaining confidence, I turned over to watch the terrifying spectacle of those murderous machines as they flattened out seemingly only feet above the trees. The scream of their engines was deafening and the turmoil of bullets striking the ground and the very branches under which we crouched seemed to deprive me of all coherent thought. But then, just as suddenly as it started, there was silence.

Shaken and frightened, I surfaced, expecting to find absolute havoc in my Flight's position. However, miracles happen, for apart from minor wounds caused by ricochets and splinters, we suffered no casualties, although some of the rucksacks dumped on the ground behind the foxholes, were now in shreds. Leaving the Flight to dig deeper, I then reported to BHQ to find that they had not been so fortunate and had lost three men.

Fortunately by then, the IO had returned and was able to give us a very sketchy picture. It was sketchy because communication between the Battalions was still not satisfactory due to the fact that the No 22 wireless sets used had a range of only 3 miles in built up areas. However, it seemed that the leading Parachute company under command of Col Frost had occupied the buildings overlooking the north end of the bridge, but the rest of the 1st Para Brigade had met with considerable opposition along their line of advance in the centre of the city. As the Divisional Commander was not at his Headquarters, it was assumed that the KOSB Battalion should continue their advance north of the railway line to secure the high ground north-west of Arnhem.

At least we had a little news of the battle and I was just walking back to the Flight, when I was caught up and grabbed by a very anxious officer.

'Quick,' he gasped, 'the Germans are preparing to attack us from the left there. Send some of your men to the northern edge of the wood so that you can cover that flank as well.'

Running back, I quickly called on Bill Sykes to follow me with No 2 Section whilst Ken Chittleburgher resited the remainder. We then took off through the trees until we reached a position where we could fire down a 300-yard wide field that separated the two wooded areas. We were just in time to see the leading platoon of Germans as they advanced in open order under the supporting fire of Spandau machine-guns.

First Blood

Siting our own Bren on the flank, we took cover behind the trees and, when the soldiers were well out in the glade, opened fire. The effect on the Germans was quite devastating. Seeing the leading men hit by bullets from an unexpected quarter, some went to ground, whilst others, in confusion, dropped their weapons and ran back to the wood which they had just left. For the first few minutes we were able to inflict casualties, but then the German machine-guns switched their fire in our direction and life became most uncomfortable. Bearing in mind that we had no ground cover, I resorted to a plan of moving a half Section at a time back into the trees to take up fresh positions 30 yards on the flank. Then when they had opened fire, the other half moved in the opposite direction. I hoped that this would fox the return fire and give the impression that our force was stronger than it really was.

The Germans did not proceed with the advance but, after a while, we were subjected to a barrage of covering fire to enable the poor chaps who had been caught out in the open to scuttle back. Eventually, both sides adopted sniping tactics against anything that moved and for the next hour, I would crawl forward, find a target, loose off a few shots and wriggle back to move to a flank.

Unfortunately, my smug satisfaction that we had saved the day for the Headquarters was soon shaken by the sound of rapid fire from the area of the farm. This now presented a problem, for if I abandoned our enfilading position, the Germans would advance once more and yet it seemed as if BHQ and my Flight again needed help. So, leaving Bill Sykes and the Bren team to continue harrassment, I took the remainder of his Section and doubled back towards the farmhouse, expecting to throw ourselves into the fray. But, as we approached, we pulled up with the realisation that the Flight weapon pits were no longer manned and, far worse, the farm was occupied by Germans! Moving to one side, both to get a better view and to find some cover for ourselves, it looked as if the whole BHQ had left in one hell of a hurry and the only British soldier remaining, was a driver fighting a lone battle by the side of his jeep. Whether he had been left behind to pull us in, I shall never know for, just at that moment, the brave man was shot and collapsed over the bonnet of his vehicle. As for my little force, I realised that we were hopelessly outnumbered and without our Bren, so I ordered the men to retire back to our original position to reform.

On assessing the situation, it looked as if the Germans had launched another attack (this time from the east) and I wrongly assumed that the KOSB second-in-command had opted to move the Headquarters together with my Flight up to the forward companies who, presumably, were still advancing slowly along the line of the railway. Accordingly, I decided to follow suit. Very cautiously, we crept forward, noting the signs of a hurried exit in the form of discarded rucksacks and equipment.

I suppose that we had advanced 600 yards, when we were virtually run into by a German NCO who was obviously making his way to the farm. I am not sure who was more surprised but fortunately, Sgt Jeff Green was the first to react and shot him. This incident made me realise that we were still not out of trouble and, sure enough, there it was in the form of a half-track vehicle which had halted at an intersection in the wood some 150 yards ahead. My first reaction was to move away to avoid detection, but then, to my delight, I realised that two of the crew were out on the ground, busily engaged in picking up loot. Here perhaps was a glorious opportunity of grabbing some transport, and so I quietly grouped the men around me in the undergrowth.

'It looks as if the crew of that half-track are busy looting, so here's a chance to capture it. Spread out on either side of Mr Sykes and keep in line with him. Take it slowly and creep from tree to tree. Then after I have thrown an impact grenade, rush in and overwhelm the crew. OK . . . lets go.'

In theory the concept was admirable and, watching the men move with extreme caution, I was sure that we would succeed. Undoubtedly we were helped because the driver, who was still in the vehicle with its engine running, was facing the other way, whilst the two men occupied with plunder were far too busy to notice anything. Our hopes of a capture were growing by the minute and my own excitement mounted as I prepared the grenade and got ready to throw. Just ten more yards, I prayed, just ten more and we will have them. Before I could move, however, the silence was shattered by a burst of Sten-gun fire from one of the pilots on the flank who, seeing two Germans in his sights, thought the opportunity was too good to miss. He killed one of the crew, but the second managed to scramble over the side of the half-track as it roared away from us at speed. Cursing our luck, I hurled the grenade after them and the whole Section opened up, but our combined fire had little effect and our big prize was lost for ever.

'Who was the bloody fool who fired?' I shouted in frustration.

'I was,' answered one of the Sergeants. 'I am sorry sir, but I thought that I had a clearer chance than you with a grenade, and I got one of them.'

'Perhaps so,' I fumed, 'but you should have waited until we were all near enough to cash in on the surprise and now we have lost everything . . . Just understand this, Sergeant Robertson, we fight as a team under orders from me. Because of your premature action we have lost the chance of capturing a half-track which could have been of value to us . . . Not only has it escaped, but the Germans will now know that we are around.'

Fortunately my anger was short-lived when the offender, abject with his apologies, managed to trip over a bramble and prostrated himself in the mud at my feet.

'OK Sergeant,' I said grinning, 'no need to grovel. We have learned a lesson, so now let's move on cautiously.'

Whilst our battles were being enacted, a major catastrophe occurred which was to have a serious effect on the battle for Arnhem. Once again, due to faulty communication, the news of the Division's change of fortune never reached the RAF squadrons in England, who proceeded to fly in accordance with the prearranged programme and 163 supply aircraft from Nos 38 & 46 Groups dropped 390 tons of badly needed food and ammunition on the original drop area which was then occupied by the Germans. Not only was this a tragic loss for the weary and hungry troops but the aircraft themselves were subjected to deadly fire from Ack-Ack guns massed there as a result of the prior captured information. The actual drop itself took only 8 minutes, during which time the crews displayed incredible bravery by forcing their way below low cloud, through a hellish barrage. In all, 13 aircraft were shot down and 97 badly damaged.

Many years later, I was to meet Flt Lt Lovemore, the navigator of our own Keevil tug crew who told me that, although their Stirling had been hit and was on fire, the pilot, Squadron Leader Davies, carried on to drop the containers and then, holding the blazing aircraft steady, ordered the crew to bail out. He crashed in flames only seconds later. It is sad to record that, during the Arnhem battle, only 7% of resupply actually reached the Division.

After the episode of the half-track, I was even more conscious that we had lost touch with the King's Own Scottish Border Battalion. To add to our problems, our supplies of food and spare ammunition were in our rucksacks at the farm, presumably in German hands. What I did not know was that, at this stage of the battle, Major-General Urquhart had reassumed command at Divisional HQ and decided to strengthen the assault of the two Parachute Battalions who were advancing towards the bridge through the city. Accordingly, he ordered the KOSBs to disengage from the enemy and to retire back to Wolfheze

Station. They were then to advance along the axis of the Utrecht-Arnhem road. Therefore, in our innocence, we were at that stage the only British soldiers north of the railway line!

As it was then dusk, I felt that there was little purpose in wandering around aimlessly and so we made use of some existing foxholes, whilst two-man teams scoured around looking for abandoned kit and rations. During the night, which was wet and cold, none of us slept and we heard the sounds of tanks and mortar fire from the south. Obviously, this was where the main body was and I resolved that we would head that way the next day.

Wednesday 20 September

With the dawn, nine cold and tired Glider Pilots edged their way southwards towards Oosterbeek with the hope of finding their own troops. The railway line we had been following now ran on an embankment about 30 foot high and I sent the leading three men over to recce if the other side was clear. They had hardly reached the rails when they came under heavy machine-gun fire.

Sergeant Jimmy Blake was hit badly and collapsed immediately across the rails, whilst the other two, although wounded, managed to escape death by diving back down the embankment. One was bleeding profusely from his face whilst the other appeared to have a bad gash in his hip. Fortunately, neither were seriously hurt and were still mobile. Leaving them to be patched up, I moved down a few yards and crawled back up the slope to a point just behind a tree, from whence I could see the prostrate Sgt Blake. Sadly, he had taken the main force of the Spandau fire in his chest and he lay with his head lodged against the far rail whilst the bulk of his body was hunched up on the track in a pool of blood. He was quite dead, although, to be sure, I called out to him, but there was no movement and any thoughts of recovering the body were quickly dispelled by another burst which straddled the corpse. Cautiously looking back, I reckoned that the Germans had set up a heavy machine-gun about 400 yards away to fire down the track on fixed lines and anyone crossing the rails would be hit.

I therefore retraced my steps and calling the pilots around, I said: 'I'm afraid that Jimmy has had it and no way we can recover his corpse. The Germans are guarding the line of this embankment and we will be looking for trouble trying to cross it here. I therefore propose to drop the plan of joining up with the troops to the south, and we will revert to the original idea of finding those attacking Arnhem from the north. So, it's back to the woods!'

Obviously at that stage, I did not have the slightest notion of what had happened to the Division nor that between us and the main body, the Germans had already welded a ring of steel, supported by tanks and self-propelled guns. Whilst I was determined to present a brave front to my men, there were occasions when I despaired to know what to do. Hence, feeling rather like a lost sheep in a quagmire of danger, I tended to become over-cautious and insisted on keeping two scouts well ahead with instructions to halt and report back on even the slightest problem.

Sure enough, it was not long before one of them was back with the news that there was a large building some 200 yards ahead which showed signs of occupation. As, in our Regimental briefing, there was a Phase 2 where Glider Pilots would assemble north of Arnhem, I crept forward hoping that we might at least meet up with some of our own. However, I was shattered by the realisation that the building at Lichtenbeek was obviously occupied by Germans as a Headquarters of sorts.

We nearly dropped into trouble there and perhaps my caution had been justified after all but, dear God, whatever was I to do now? I had tried to join up with those battalions advancing to the south along the Utrecht–Arnhem road without success and, in moving north, had run into further difficulties. It was now D + 4 and my small party was tired, cold and without food and, under those miserable circum-stances, it was a credit to the spirit of the pilots that they kept going so cheerfully.

Happily, on that day our luck changed, and my problem was soon to be solved by a member of the Dutch resistance movement. After our near miss at the German HQ, I had retraced our steps deep into the trees once more. The woods themselves seemed to have been planted with paths intersecting the plantation. We were spread out resting in the undergrowth, when a man in farm clothes cycled past. We had all remained very quiet, but he must have seen something because, after 20 yards, he dismounted and dumping his bicycle, walked back towards us, softly calling 'Hello, hello.'

Leaving the others, I rose to meet a strong and sturdy labourer, with an open rosy face which was wreathed in smiles. He came towards me with both his arms stretched out wide to embrace me with a bear hug. He couldn't speak a word of English, but gabbled away in Dutch, spitting on the ground in an expression of disgust when mentioning the 'Boche'. Somehow we managed to communicate in sign language and the outcome was he persuaded us to stay hidden whilst he fetched someone to help. He would only be 30 minutes and, with that, he mounted his bicycle and pedalled off, waving happily.

EIGHT

DUTCH RESISTANCE

Rescue

I discussed the gist of our conversation with the men who agreed that
the sorely needed help might now be available. However, to be
absolutely sure we were not getting ourselves into a trap, we dispersed
even more widely whilst I hid behind a tree on the other side of the
path. Fortunately, our fears were unfounded, because he came back
with a well-dressed man who promptly shook me by the hand and, in
reasonable English, introduced himself as Dr Coeberg.

'I am Captain Morrison,' I replied. 'I have with me seven Glider
Pilots. We have had a fight with the Germans and have been separated
from our unit. Can you help us to rejoin the Airborne troops, and can
you stitch up the wounds of a couple of my chaps here?'

'Yes, of course, but I must tell you that I am not a doctor but a vet.
Anyway, let's have a look at them. Ah yes,' he grunted inspecting the
damage. 'They were lucky they are only deep surface wounds and I
can soon fix them up. Now about getting you back to your troops, that
is going to be more difficult. In my job I am allowed to travel around
and, from friends, I understand that there has been some delay in the
join up with the army from the south. Also, the Boche have brought up
Tiger tanks to prevent the main Airborne body from re-inforcing those
who still hold one end of the bridge, so your friends have now dug in
around Oosterbeek to await relief from "Monty".'

'Don't worry,' he said with a grin, 'they will be here tomorrow. In
the meantime we will look after you and when they take Arnhem, you
can help us to finish off those German swine.'

I discussed his idea with my pilots who had now gathered on the edge
of our conversation and we agreed that, for a matter of 36 hours or so,
it had merit. Accordingly, we split into three parties to be spirited away
into private homes. I took with me the two Staff Sergeants who had
been wounded earlier that morning and went along with Dr Coeberg,
whilst the farm labourer gathered up the others to leave with the assurance that we would keep in touch and reassemble when the time was
appropriate. As they moved away, happier with the prospect of being

sheltered by a family who, like so many other Hollanders, risked their lives hiding Airborne soldiers, I was prompted to wave and call out, 'See you chaps, just keep out of trouble'.

I was still watching them out of sight when I was conscious of a hand on my shoulder – it was our new friend. 'Don't worry Captain, they will be safe. We must now get to my house. Please follow a little way behind me and if we run into trouble – hide. I will find you later.' He then turned and strode away, leaving us to trail behind, still conscious of the danger that surrounded us.

Dr 'Schef', as I came to know him, was a vet who practised from a small surgery in his house. He was a quiet, unassuming man, strong and upright in build and with a burning patriotism that was reflected in his voice whenever he spoke of his country. He had been involved with the 'underground movement' since the early days of German occupation and, although not directly active with subversion, he served as a 'transit' house as visits to his surgery provided a good cover. His feeling for his country was completely shared by his attractive wife Thea, who had also been active in caring for those on the run.

Upon approaching a large three storey home, we were told to wait in the trees at the end of the garden, whilst he went indoors to check that all was clear and also to warn his wife that she should expect visitors. Her reaction was immediate, for with a flurry of skirts, she ran to welcome us with a gay and happy greeting. Leading us up the paved path towards the back of the house, she chatted away in a mixture of Dutch and English, excited at being able to look after 'the heroes'. We went through a small porch, then entered a large, warm kitchen, where we were introduced with great solemnity to two pretty little blonde girls who shyly shook our hands. Whilst our host took off the two casualties to clean and stitch up their wounds, I realised how wonderful it was to be in a home again, and to feel the comfort of a fire.

'When did you last eat?' asked Thea.

'I really can't remember, I suppose about four days ago,' I replied.

'You poor things.'

The family then set about preparing steaming hot coffee with fresh white bread, spread liberally with real butter and plum jam. It was fantastic, and I am afraid that the three of us gobbled down that welcome food, much to the amusement of the children. Finally, when replete and feeling a little ashamed of our gluttonous exhibition, we sat down across the table to Schef and his wife to review our position.

'We are delighted to have you with us,' he declared. 'But for your sake and ours, it is important that you understand our problems and act accordingly. First, remember that not all Dutchmen are friends. Sadly there are those who quite openly side with the Germans and will not hesitate to let them know that we are housing soldiers. If this happens, I will be shot and my wife and family left destitute. It is imperative therefore that you do not attempt to leave this house without a guide and, during the day, remain hidden in your room and not be seen at the window. Right now, the Germans are very nervous and are introducing all sorts of restrictive measures to curb any support to the "invasion" by the locals. They have already evacuated the houses around Oosterbeek and there is a rumour that they want to clear Arnhem.

'Now, about your accommodation, we have a large attic, where we presently store old furniture, trunks, books and other junk. If my wife gives you a mattress each and some blankets, it should be quite comfortable. It also has the benefit that it can only be entered from some steep stairs with a door at the bottom which we can lock from either side – so there is little to fear from a chance visitor. As I see it, the main problem will be the use of the lavatory and here I think the best thing would be for you to go to the bathroom first thing in the morning and last at night. We have a commode up there which you can have for emergencies, so that should be all right. We normally have our main meal in the evening and it would give you a break to join us here in the kitchen which is as safe as any room in the house. Other food will be brought to you by my wife, for again I must stress that you must not be seen by anyone outside.

'Now as far as news of the assault is concerned, I will make a point of finding out about "Monty" and his progress and particularly about your own Division and we can then make a plan to suit the situation . . . OK?'

'OK,' I replied. 'We are most grateful for the help that you and your wife are giving us and we realise the danger to which you may be exposed if we are seen. You also have our promise that we will obey your wishes . . . As far as future plans are concerned, I am sure that you will understand that I worry about my Flight, and if it is humanly possible, would like to rejoin my men as soon as I can.'

'Don't worry, we will have you back together directly it is safe . . . Now I guess you are tired and could catch up with some sleep.' With that, both he and his wife led the way to the attic, which was certainly roomy and warm and it was not long before they brought up the mattresses and blankets which we moved into a central space which we had cleared. Then, with the assurance that we would be woken up for supper, they left us to flop down and, within seconds, the three of us were fast asleep. Thus began our brief but happy stay in their wonderful care.

My two companions were both happy, outgoing characters who had already shrugged off the discomfort of their wounds. Don Donaldson, the elder, was a heavily-built fellow, standing over 6 ft tall, with a pleasant open face and a calm disposition. He had volunteered for gliders after he had been wounded during a Commando raid. It so happened that, whilst he was still in hospital, his particular unit had been transferred overseas, and rather than await the outcome of a future posting, he submitted his application to become a 'flying soldier'. Fortunately, the medical examination to which he had been subjected at Oxford, took little cognisance of a healthy young man with two toes missing on his right foot. He was equally lucky that the process of intake into the Regiment had been delayed, due mainly to the lack of flying training facilities, because it gave him a further month to become completely fit and capable of coping with the rigorous basic training to which all new entrants were subjected. During the short *mêlée* on the railway embankment, a sharp stone, kicked up by a bullet, had cut him high on the cheek. An inch higher would have taken out his eye, and he was indeed fortunate to get away with a deep gash which could be stitched. I believe that he was quite proud of his duelling scar!

The second Staff Sergeant was Stephen Rogers, nicknamed by the Flight as 'Roger the Lodger' or 'Sexy Steve'. He hailed from Brentford and was apprenticed in his father's electrical repair business. Whilst he had promised the family that he would qualify as an electrician, I am sure that his sole ambition was to become a professional footballer, particularly, as before the war, he had excelled in the Colts team. He was a bright and breezy young man, with crinkly fair hair and blue eyes. He always seemed to be smiling, even in the most difficult circumstances, and his main concern was not the bullet wound in his thigh and the resulting stiffness, but the fact that his battle dress was torn.

I was still out to the world when, at 8 o'clock, Dr Schef shook me awake. He had a razor and brush in his hand. 'I thought that you might like to have a wash and shave before the meal, which will be ready soon.'

Taking it in turns with the hot water and 'equipment', it was not long before the three of us looked reasonably presentable. The fillip that this gave to our morale was unbelievable. Smiling from ear to ear, we crept down to the kitchen to be met with shouts of joy and laughter at the transformation.

The meal of vegetable stew was a happy one, and I was left in no doubt that our hosts were delighted to repay their 'heroes' for all the hardships and suffering that we had endured in our efforts to free the Dutch people from their bondage. Schef produced a bottle of schnapps and, having sent the children to bed, insisted on us telling them, in detail, about our experiences. Whether it was the drink or the warmth of the room, I do not know, but by about 10 o'clock we were all having the greatest difficulty in keeping awake. Realising this, our hosts promptly packed us off upstairs once more.

Thursday 21 September

The following morning, after a good night's sleep, I felt wonderful and my pleasure was heightened by the sight of two lovely little girls, looking very fresh and bright, each holding a plate of bread and butter for us, whilst their mother followed with coffee and marmalade.

'I hope that you all slept well and are feeling rested,' she said with a smile. 'Schef left early this morning to cycle over to help a local farmer, but he hopes to be back by 2 o'clock. He will make a point of finding out about the Division and also news of Monty's progress but he again asks you to be patient and to keep away from the window . . . Now, is there anything that you want? No. Well, I will send one of the girls up later this morning and if you think of something she can call me.' They then left with a cheery wave.

Having finished our breakfast, we had a chance of looking around our living quarters which was an area built under the rafters of the roof that had been boarded in to make a long room with a window on each side. Whilst the windows were double curtained, it was possible to stand on the flank and catch a glimpse of the road, but, in keeping with instructions, we were very careful not to be seen. As indicated by our host, the room was full of junk, but this in itself provided considerable amusement in paging through ancient photograph albums and old copies of magazines, some of which were in English.

When Schef returned that afternoon, he came up to our room and sat on the floor.

'The British troops are still holding the north end of the bridge, but from all reports the street fighting in the city is proving very costly. The bulk of the Division is located around Oosterbeek. As far as the Armoured Division is concerned, they have occupied Eindhoven but are held up because the bridge at Son had been blown. Fighting is pretty heavy but I am sure that the Guards will soon break through, so we will not have long to wait. Incidentally, I had a bit of a problem with the German military police who wanted to know where I was going on my bicycle. I showed them my official pass as a vet and suggested that even in war, farmers had to produce food and milk even for the occupying forces, and animals still became sick. I don't think that they liked it and warned me to keep away.'

That evening we again enjoyed a stew, for which Thea apologised, and listened with interest whilst Schef told us of life in Holland, both before and after the Germans came. Again we were not late but as we had no lighting, we had a small problem when we finally came to bed down for the night. However, we soon became orientated and after a certain amount of happy banter were fast asleep.

Friday 22 September

The morning was devoted to cleaning our weapons and taking stock of ammunition, which was sadly depleted. I had an American airborne automatic rifle with two magazines each of eight rounds and a couple of Mills grenades whilst my two companions, both with a Sten, were down to one full magazine each. Hardly a formidable fighting force.

Although we were made most welcome and comfortable, by this time I began to worry about the rest of my Flight, who presumably were still attached to the KOSB battalion. So, that evening, I approached our host quietly.

'Schef, earlier I told you how we had been separated from the rest of our Flight and I am worried that I should be with them. Do you think it would be possible for me to make my way through the German lines especially if I went right round to the west?'

'It might be possible,' was the curt reply, 'but a damn stupid idea. For goodness sake John, what is the hurry? The British armoured corps are only 17 km away . . . an hour or two and they must break through anytime now. In any case, surely you have other officers in your Flight who can cope without you?'

'Oh they can manage all right, but from your reports, the Division has withdrawn into a defensive area and are being shelled and attacked by tanks and my place is with my men. I just can't sit around here in comfort knowing that they are in trouble. Not even a day or two.'

'I suppose that I can understand your feelings, although I still consider that you will be taking an unnecessary risk. We will be sorry to lose you, but if you insist upon going, there is only one man who can get you through . . . that's Jan. He knows the woods like the back of his hand – he's brave as a lion and will be delighted to help. So I'll meet you halfway. If the army is not here by dusk tomorrow, Jan will take you. In the meantime I will warn him to decide upon the best route.'

Saturday 23 September

Night Skirmish

Despite Schef's optimism, we waited in vain for the sound of our approaching tanks and therefore resolved to set forth. Jan, the forrester who originally found us, arrived at the Coeberg's home before dusk

74

and the three of us, having said a fond farewell to the family, left hopefully to rejoin our own troops. Our guide was happy to assist and, knowing the area intimately, set off at a brisk pace along one of the many paths that intercepted the extensive woods. Unfortunately, rain had set in and, because we had no groundsheets, it was not long before our Airborne smocks were wet through, but the prospect of meeting up with the rest of the Flight overshadowed any discomfort.

With the fading light, Jan obviously wished to make as much progress as possible, although it was this over-confidence that nearly ended in disaster for us all. I suppose we had been walking for about an hour when we came to a dust road and had halted just short of it whilst Jan crossed over to see if all was clear. However, standing there, I became conscious of the noise of trucks approaching from our left. Quickly pulling back 15 yards, we flattened ourselves in the undergrowth where we lay with bated breath and watched. Three large lorries drove slowly past the very spot where we had been standing and came to a halt. Then, with much shouting and swearing, the tailboards were dropped and about half a company of Germans jumped down to form up in Sections.

Hardly daring to raise my head, I tried desperately to think of a plan to extricate ourselves in the event of them advancing in our direction. Although it was fairly dark, we would not stand a chance if they found us. Using signs to my companions, I indicated that, at the first opportunity, we should retire back along the original path. However as I lay there waiting for the moment to move, it dawned on me that the Germans were lining up on the far side of their trucks, facing Oosterbeek and that this would present a heaven-sent opportunity to use the blackness of the wood to our advantage.

Accordingly, I motioned the pilots towards me and whispered:

'We have got to get the hell out of this, so individually, we will make our way back along the path behind us and we will meet at the next intersection. Before we go, I don't see why we should not give Jerry something to think about. I have a couple of grenades which I will try to lob over the top of the trucks. You, Don, take up a position 20 yards to my right and you, Steve, 20 yards to my left. When both grenades explode, stand up and fire one short burst at the front and rear Sections. Just one burst mind you and then run for your lives. Do you understand? OK get moving.'

With that, gripping my rifle, I slowly crawled forward towards the edge of the road. There in front of me and only 20 yards away, was the second of the trucks with the other vehicles parked just in front and behind. From the considerable noise and shouting that was going on,

I concluded that, either the NCOs were nervous or, alternatively, they were dealing with inexperienced troops. Whatever the case, they were clearly not expecting British soldiers in the area and the racket covered any sound that we might have made. After waiting a couple of minutes for the others to reach their positions, I grounded my rifle and then very slowly, moved forward to stand behind a tree.

Taking one of the two grenades from my pocket, I pulled out the pin and lobbed it as far as I could in the direction of the last truck. This was followed immediately by my second which I was able to throw over the canopy of the truck in front of me, before dropping down to lie with my head buried behind a bank. I counted up to seven but nothing happened. Hell I thought, surely they had been primed. Then, as if in answer, came the first explosion, then the second in quick succession. Shrapnel was flying everywhere, splattering the trucks and the trees under which we crouched; the ensuing shouts of pain gave proof that at least someone had been hit. By now, Don and Steve were up and shooting into the area, hosing their fire where the soldiers had assembled. I then added my own contribution before turning and beating a hasty retreat down the path.

I had hardly gone twenty yards before sheer Bedlam broke loose, for the Germans in their panic were firing in all directions and not taking the slightest notice of their NCOs who were trying to direct fire to where they thought the attack was emanating. The flash of their rifles and the *Wheeeeze* of the bullets as they ricocheted through the trees added urgency to my flight and even three minutes later, when I had caught up with the others, the Germans were still fighting off the 'assault'. I shall never know the 'score' for our little effort, but, at the time, our spirits soared as we clapped each other on the back, giggling like small children. At least we had re-entered the battle and might have disrupted, even temporarily, an enemy plan.

Ultimately, of course, our joy subsided, particularly when we realised that we had lost Jan who was on the other side of the road. Was he all right or had he been on the receiving end of the German fire? Whatever the answer, there was nothing that we could do about it now and our wonderful idea of reaching our own had 'had it'. Standing there in the darkness, our situation suddenly became impossible.

'Blast the Germans,' I murmured, 'now we are back where we started . . . and lost! Well, I don't think we should wander about aimlessly, so there is only one thing to do, we will move deeper into the woods and stick it out. Then, at dawn, attempt to find our way back to Coeberg's home and try again tomorrow.'

We quickly moved off the path and found a little hollow into which we huddled together closely to give each other warmth and, taking turns to watch, tried to sleep.

Sunday 24 September

I was awake when the first streaks of light heralded a very wet grey day and arousing Don and Steve, we had a brief shivering conference as to the direction we should take. Fortunately, after moving cautiously northwards, we were able to recognise landmarks and eventually, cold, damp but still excited from our little escapade, three Glider Pilots were crouching in the bushes at the end of the Coeberg's garden.

Our reception from the children was rapturous, and in welcoming us back to his care, Dr Schef confirmed what we feared, namely that the British relieving forces had failed to break through and the Division had adopted a holding role. In the meantime, the Germans had brought up further tanks and artillery to completely surround our men.

'Never mind,' said Schef, 'be patient and tomorrow or the next day, Monty will be here.'

It was hard to accept this advice and I politely told him that I would like to discuss our situation with my pilots, particularly as I was also conscious that we continued to be a potential threat to his family. However, the decision was really taken for us by the happy and most welcome arrival of our faithful guide, Jan.

He came into our room upstairs with a shout of joy and shook us all vigorously by the hand to explain, through Schef, that when he realised that the German trucks had stopped near where he had left us, he had crept away to complete a circuit round to the left in order to pick us up again. He had hardly recrossed the road about 200 yards to the east, when our grenades exploded and all the firing began. With great delight he confirmed that the Boche had panicked and had loosed off hundreds of rounds in all directions before they realised that it was not a sustained attack. He had not been near enough to see if there had been casualties, but said that there had been a good deal of shouting for help.

He had realised that there was little hope of finding us in that *mêlée* and so he had stayed the rest of the night in a forester's shelter. The following morning, thinking that we might still be around, he had quietly reccied along the line of the road only to find the whole area still swarming with Germans. Speaking with feeling, he confessed that it had now become too dangerous to try and break through the German lines at that point and it would be wiser to give him 24 hours to find out if there could be an approach from the west.

Tuesday 26 September

Sadly, the next day when he arrived, he came with the startling news that, as there was no immediate hope of the British armour breaking through to the bridge, the survivors of the 1st Airborne Division at Oosterbeek had actually been ferried back across the

Rhine overnight, leaving behind the wounded and little units like ourselves who had been separated from the main force. Understandably, we were terribly depressed for we were now stranded once more.

'What happened to the famous Guards Armoured Brigade?' questioned Don. 'Surely they could have forced a way through. What about our Division who expected to fight two days, and now it is nine? What has gone wrong?'

'I know it looks pretty grim Don,' I replied. 'But there must have been a very good reason for abandoning the plan and our chaps must have taken heavy punishment! Look it's nearly news time on the BBC. Maybe there will be a message for those left behind.'

We moved to the kitchen and huddled round a small radio to listen to a report that was still full of optimism. It referred blandly to the rescue of the 'airborne heroes' who, against overwhelming odds, had held up the Germans for ten days, thereby giving XXX Corps the opportunity of reaching the south bank of the river. Right now these very forces were preparing for an assault across the Rhine and the final battle was only a matter of days.

I suppose that, in times of uncertainty, one tends to grasp encouragement from any source and it certainly looked as if the long-awaited attack was imminent. With this in mind, we decided to take the advice of our hosts and stay put. However, with the cessation of fighting around Oosterbeek, it was not long before the Germans directed their efforts into mopping up pockets of resistance, picking up stragglers and, what was bad for our hosts, rounding up those members of the public who had openly declared their support for the British. Directives had already been issued for the complete evacuation of the Arnhem area, and during the following days a total of 90,000 Hollanders were forced to vacate their homes. Quite obviously, our family was in danger and had no other course but to seek shelter with friends who had a farm near Apeldoorn to the north.

'What about our joining the hundreds of refugees,' I asked. 'I don't like the idea of hanging around here. If we could borrow some clothes, I reckon that we could live on the country for a while.'

'I am afraid not,' replied Schef. 'The German police have already covered that escape route and have set up road blocks everywhere with orders to shoot anyone without a pass. No, your safest plan is to sit tight until Monty arrives. I know that I have been wrong about the breakthrough but it must come soon. I promise you that if it hasn't happened in seven days, I will arrange to get you out.'

Early the next day they loaded up a lightweight trailer which Schef used to tow behind his bicycle and, after a tearful farewell from the lovely children, the family prepared to move off, but not before Thea had handed to us her reserve of food, which she had unearthed from a secret hiding place.

As we all gathered round the Coebergs, I expressed our sincere feelings. 'You have both been absolutely marvellous looking after us and no matter what happens in the next few days, we will never forget your kindness. Now, just look after yourselves and may God bless you.'

Schef embraced us warmly and Thea, with tears streaming down her face, kissed us farewell. We watched them move off, with the children sitting on top of the cases in the trailer, and as they joined the road we ran up to the attic to catch a fleeting glance of that wonderful family. It was now a case of biding our time until the arrival of the British Army.

Betrayal and Capture

At dawn two days later, two trucks full of soldiers pulled up outside the house and surrounded the building. It seems that quislings, realising that the Germans had foiled the Airborne attack, were now making sure of their own safety by betraying their countrymen and had reported the Coebergs. We were asleep at the time and the first that we knew of the raid was when we heard the glass of the front door smashed, followed by the staccato of Schmeiser firing.

'What the hell is going on?' cursed Don as he rushed to the window. 'Christ, the bloody Huns are here. There are hundreds of them swarming all around the house. What can we do?'

'Well we can't take on that number, just the three of us and with no 'ammo', I answered. 'Our only hope is to hide here in the attic and pray that they don't find us. Steve, quickly check that the bottom door is locked and Don and I will dump our kit behind the boarding.'

Then, scared and worried, we hid in our prearranged spots in the vain hope that they might not find us. In awesome anticipation, I lay between the couch and the wall, hardly daring to breathe. I could hear soldiers shouting to each other and firing into empty rooms. Eventually someone tried the attic door and finding it locked, burst it open with automatic fire. Then came the orders urging the men up the stairs.

In desperation I grovelled behind my cover hoping that I would not be seen, but from subsequent shouting, I realised that the two Staff Sergeants had been found and it was shortly to be me, when, with a gun poked viciously into my ribs, I was herded into the centre of the room. There we stood in our underclothes, our hands above our heads, appalled and frustrated at having been captured. All the effort and, far more important, all the risks taken by our Dutch family had been for naught. I glanced over at Steve who was looking as sick at heart as I felt, and slowly shook my head. There was nothing we could do now but to stick it out and hope there might be a chance of escape later.

Finally, when the Germans who had continued their search of the attic declared it to be clear, we were ordered to dress after which, with much pushing and shouting, we were frog-marched downstairs into the back of one of the trucks accompanied by a number of 'cocky' *Grune Polizei* who were obviously very pleased with themselves at having found us. Ten minutes later, we drove off and, after a comparatively short journey, arrived at a large mansion which I recognised as the Headquarters that we had seen in our earlier travels.

Directly our truck halted outside the entrance, the tailboard was dropped and with shouts of '*Raus-raus*', one of the guards indicated that we should debus. This we did midst more pushing and shouting and were led up some steps into a bare room where we were handed over to two uncouth-looking soldiers who, once more, went through the process of searching us. Again this was done with unnecessary roughness as if to invite reaction and then with a final shove I was propelled towards the far wall and told to sit down.

It took me a few minutes to regain my composure but eventually, looking around, I noticed that, on the other side of the room were two dishevelled and exhausted parachutists together with a wretched civilian who had obviously been picked up whilst looking after them. He had taken a terrible battering from the hands of his captors and lay, propped against the wall, quietly sobbing to himself whilst clutching a wound at the top of his leg.

For a while I watched this poor man, who was obviously in great pain, and had blood seeping through his torn trousers onto the floor. Eventually, as the guards were outside, I crawled over to him and, still kneeling, took out and undid my field dressing. I was about to staunch the flow of blood when, without warning, I received a tremendous crack on the side of my head with a rifle butt which sent me sprawling on the floor. Seeing red in more senses than one, I whipped round and in blind anger, grabbed the knees of my attacker, a large and vicious looking SS *Korporal*, only to be struck again on the head which all but laid me out.

By then, the other guard had run into the room and the two of them, standing over my prostrate body, proceeded to kick the daylights out of my ribs with their hobnailed boots. All the time, they were shouting in German whilst I, dizzy and helpless, feebly waved the field dressing that was still clutched in my hand, in the direction of the Dutchman. Fortunately, the commotion prompted a passing officer to ask what the trouble was and the two paused in their kicking to explain. This respite gave me the chance to get to my feet and with sign language point out that I was only trying to apply a field dressing to the wounded man's leg. Grabbing the bandage from my hand, the officer flung it at the wretched civilian who, by then was quite terrified, and with a curt '*Kom*' indicated that I should follow him. This I did, 'assisted' by one of the guards who speeded my faltering footsteps with prods from his rifle, until we arrived at a room where the walls were covered with maps.

'Now I'm for it,' I thought, 'this is where the questioning starts.' Fortunately, however, the purpose of the trip was to find someone who could speak English and through this interpreter, tell me that, as an officer, I should have been segregated and in any case, I had no right to speak to the 'Dutch traitor'. The outcome was that my first night in captivity was spent in the corner of a room in the company of six SS officers, but without my boots.

I must confess that, at that moment, I was feeling very sorry for myself. I had a thick ear, my head was aching terribly and I couldn't breathe deeply without a searing pain in my ribs. My new companions, obviously elated with their success of recovering the bridgehead, magnanimously tried to make life easier for me by offering cigarettes and hot black coffee. However, as their efforts at sign conversation became very one-sided, they slowly faltered and were soon snoring.

Unhappily for me, sleep would not come for I was mentally over-whelmed with remorse. All the effort, the hours of waiting and anxiety, the continuous strain of battle and the subsequent feeling of exhaustion were all for nothing. I just could not understand why the grand concept had failed. We had been so confident of victory and yet, where was the magnificent Armoured Division with the cream of the British regiments?

Where was the promised air support? And how the hell did they expect lightly armed troops to cope with Tiger tanks? These and a hundred other questions raced through my mind as I lay in that room. Where had I failed? Perhaps I had been too complacent and should have escaped to the north when we knew that the Division had been pulled out and yet, bearing in mind that we were all so sure that it would only be a matter of days before our formidable army would break through, to stay seemed to have been the right decision. How were we found? Had we been careless and seen, or had quislings known the Coebergs were hiding Airborne soldiers?

I suppose, on reflection, I should have been grateful to have been spared and thanked God for the blessing of life, but even so, I must confess that the prospect of being a prisoner filled me with foreboding. Fortunately, after this short spell of self-pity, my personal pride surfaced. I was not beaten although, admittedly, I had had a setback. I was 'down' but certainly not 'out'. There and then I promised myself that somehow, I would win through and with that comforting thought, I too started snoring.

Journey into Germany

Early next morning, I was woken by the interpreter with my boots, a slice of rye bread and a Mess tin of steaming black coffee. He brought me the news that I was to be sent to an Interrogation Centre. We were to travel by train, but I was not to try to escape, otherwise I would be shot. Having put on my boots, I painfully got to my feet and 'set about' the meagre breakfast. I was ravenous and within seconds the bread had been consumed. The interpreter seemed amused at this 'disappearance trick' and promptly replenished my plate with two more slices.

'Thank you very much,' I said, 'I was hungry.'

'You looked it,' he replied with a grin. 'Anyway, you are the lucky one – for you the war is over! For me, what will the future bring? Now will you come with me.' He led the way outside where I found a mixed group of Airborne soldiers, together with a number of aircrew who had been shot down.

I suppose there were about 56 of us altogether, a motley crew of dejected men who somehow had been picked up at a time when hopes of victory had still been strong. We stood around in silent groups, until assembled in four lines with the officers to the right, so that a *Wehrmacht* Sergeant could make his way down the ranks, recording our names in a notebook. Looking sideways, I caught sight of Don and Steve and with a thumbs up sign, indicated that all was well. Their cheerful response was heartening and brought comfort to an otherwise gloomy prospect.

The bookwork finished, we were counted twice and the interpreter summoned to repeat the instructions given to me earlier. Then with shouted commands, we turned right and with guards in the front, to the side and at the rear of the column, moved off to a railway siding about ten miles to the east of Arnhem. My own progress was fairly painful for I was sure that the wretched SS guards had cracked a rib, but it could have been worse. One of the bunch, a New Zealand pilot, had broken his collar-bone after baling out of his aircraft and, for him, the pushing and shoving must have been sheer agony.

The senior officer of our little group was a Major in the Parachute Regiment who had been wounded and put into hospital. One night he had walked out unnoticed and had taken refuge in an empty house, but his freedom had been short lived when he was spotted scrounging for food. Despite a nasty chest wound, he was still very much in command and insisted that we marched smartly and in step.

'Come on lads,' he called out 'put a brave face on things and show these 'krauts' that we still have spirit. Now what about a song!' He started to sing 'It's a long way to Tipperary'. We were marching through a little hamlet at the time and obviously some of the Dutch people, thinking that the British Army had broken through, rushed out of their houses waving happily, only to be sadly disillusioned upon seeing the guards.

Shortly afterwards, we halted for a break and sat down by the side of the road, whilst the guards faced inwards with their rifles at the ready. Once again the locals showed their compassion and complete disregard for their personal safety, bringing boxes of apples which they handed to us with smiles and messages of good luck.

Eventually, after four hours of marching, we turned off the tarmac to head for a small siding where we lined up by the side of a decrepit old passenger carriage which was to be our home for the next seven days. It had been converted for the transportation of PoWs as all the windows were sealed and barred and both the corridor and outside doors could be locked securely. Accommodation worked out at eight to a compartment, whilst the guards were allocated those at the front and rear of the carriage.

Before boarding, we were instructed to file past a table where each man was handed a tin mug filled with hot vegetable broth and a chunk of rye bread. After we had consumed our 'meal', we returned to the table to wash the mugs in a corrugated iron bath prior to dropping them into a sack. We then directed our steps towards some latrines and finally lined up once more to be counted again. Having climbed into our respective compartments, the NCO in charge then ticked off the names of the prisoners and, having checked that the corridor was secure, he locked the outside doors.

Apart from the Parachute Major, the rest of the chaps in my compartment were aircrew. They told of the harrowing experience of the 'resupply operation' during which they had to fly, below cloud, through a murderous concentration of 'ack-ack' fire. Not one of the aircraft had diverted to avoid being hit, but ploughed through a veritable wall of shrapnel. They were a grand bunch and we were able to pass the dreary hours recounting our individual experiences – dreary hours they certainly were because it was nearly dark before an engine coupled us onto a goods train which ultimately set off on its ponderous way.

The journey itself was a nightmare for, as a 'third rate special', we were constantly shunted onto secondary lines for hours on end. I guess that the direct trip would have taken a half a day at the most but, presumably, due to Allied bombing, we seemed to be travelling throughout Germany. Firstly we headed down to Cologne, then changed direction north to Münster and finally it was then a long trek south-east to our final destination – Lundburg *Stalag* 12 A.

For some reason, there had been no provision to feed the 56 prisoners and apart from three hand-outs of a loaf per compartment, we literally survived on the water we drank at the stops. Protests to the senior German NCO were greeted with a shrug of the shoulders with palms extended upwards, or the symbolic display of empty pockets.

Horsa gliders lie abandoned behind the trees in this photograph of Pegasus Bridge, taken from the east. *(Imperial War Museum; B5288)*

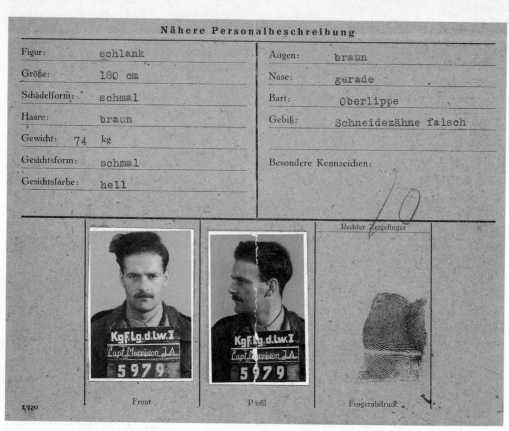

The author's identity pass made out when he entered *Stalag Luft 1*. 'It shows how I felt.'

The Russian pass states – 'By authority of Colonel ZCHERVYNICK, Commander of Barth District, the bearer is authorized to be in the Barth Area between the hours of 1000 and 2100.'

NINE

INTERROGATION

Luftwaffe Centre

At last, seven weary days later, hungry, dirty and unshaven, we left our mobile prison and marched to what appeared to be a transit camp. There at least we were given a meal of vegetable stew but any ideas of a wash and bed were quickly dispelled. Upon roll call, the eight aircrew and I were loaded into a truck under guard and driven off to the Interrogation Centre at Frankfurt. There we were to pass through the ominous gates of a prison camp that were overlooked on either side by postern towers from which floodlights brilliantly lit up a wire enclosure. We were then checked and officially handed over to our new masters.

After a while, the Camp Commandant, a *Luftwaffe Oberst Lnt*, came out of his office and addressed the small group in perfect English:

> 'This is an Airforce Interrogation Centre where you will be asked questions by airforce officers. Your length of stay here will depend on your answers, and I do advise you to assist in the task of verifying your identity. Only when we are satisfied will you be transferred to a proper prisoner-of-war camp. In the meantime, let me warn you that this centre is surrounded by an electric fence and anyone attempting to escape will be electrocuted.'

We were then called individually for recording and a thorough search. I was made to strip completely whilst my uniform, boots and all clothing were examined. Every personal item, such as my watch, pen and number tag were taken and placed in an envelope which was duly marked with my name, rank and number. Finally, I was subjected to a body search which was both unpleasant and degrading. When satisfied that I had no escape aids, I was permitted to dress, except for my boots, and a guard then led me via the lavatory, to a corridor in which there were a line of cells. Upon coming to a door marked A8 he stood aside to usher me into a dark interior in which I could just discern a bed, before the door was slammed shut and locked, leaving me in complete darkness.

Feeling my way forward, I groped and found the edge of the bed and lay down to stare into pitch black surroundings. Then, after an hour or so, I dropped onto my knees to offer up a fervent prayer for my deliverance and to ask for moral strength of mind for the ordeal which was to follow.

Despite the previous seven days of comparative inactivity, I felt absolutely exhausted and soon fell asleep fully clothed, waking early next morning when the shutters were opened. In the darkness of the previous night, I had the feeling that I was incarcerated in a packing case and upon inspection in the light of day, it really didn't seem much larger. In fact, my cell was just over 6 ft long by 5 ft wide, in which a lifting shelf-bed occupied one complete side, leaving only a narrow space between the edge and the opposite wall. On this shelf there was a thin mattress and a 'tatty' blanket and the whole could be hinged up and secured to provide extra space. At one end of the cell was a door which closed flush with the wall and which, at four feet from the floor, had a small ledge in front of a sliding partition. Right at the top of the end wall was a barred window about 18 inches square, through which the sun's rays were now penetrating.

I had hardly sized up my meagre 'box' when there was a bang on the door. The partition slid back and a tin plate with a thick slice of rye bread together with a mug of *ersatz* coffee were pushed onto the ledge. Having learnt a lesson from the train journey, I decided to save half my rations and kept the plate but after 30 minutes, there was another bang on the door and the partition slid back. As no empty plate nor mug were on the ledge, it was promptly shut and, as punishment, I was to miss the noon bread issue. Fortunately, I was 'forgiven' by supper time when I was to partake of a watery cabbage soup with a slice of bread.

'Well,' I thought, 'if this is to be the extent of my food intake, I must work out a programme of exercises that will keep me fit without using too much energy.' These exercises I conscientiously did three times a day and I am sure that the regimentation of action assisted greatly in creating a strong mental attitude.

Gestapo Take Over

My first interrogation was about 3 o'clock the following afternoon when I was ushered into a bare room in which the only pieces of furniture were a table covered with files and two chairs. Sitting behind the table were two officers and I was shaken to realise that they were certainly not *Luftwaffe* but *Gestapo*! With a curt sign, I was ordered to stand to attention exactly three feet in front of the senior one who was a sallow-looking individual with a scrawny neck that supported a pinched, pock-marked, blotchy face. I suppose that he was about 40 years old, and had a mean disposition which predominated his whole approach.

For two interminable minutes he stared at me with pale blue eyes that glistened behind a pair of rimless spectacles. His mouth was taut and stern and, when he finally spoke, the words seemed to shoot out in a series of staccato phrases.

'No 88880 Captain J.A. Morrison?' he queried, raising his pale eyebrows.

'That's correct,' I replied.

Picking up a heavy round ruler, he slammed it on the table. 'You will address me as *Herr* Major,' came the first whiplash. 'What are you? How did you come to be found in Arnhem?'

As I was wearing wings on my battle dress, I pointed to them. '*Herr* Major . . . I am a Glider Pilot and I fought in the battle for Arnhem.'

'So that's your story is it?' he sneered. 'You are a liar. A filthy liar. The British were defeated on 26 September and today's date is 9 October. So where have you been for 14 days?' he snapped.

I forced myself to look at my interrogator straight in the eye and patiently explained. 'I and my men were separated from our unit during the fighting and were captured immediately after the battle had ended. We were held as prisoners at Battalion Headquarters for a while and then marched into Germany where we were put on a train which took eight days to reach *Stalag* 12 A.' Again, I was subjected to a stare while the second officer, a fat-looking slug, painstakingly recorded my reply.

'I don't believe a word you say. Not a single word,' he shouted hitting the table once more with the ruler. 'We have proof that after Arnhem, the British parachuted agents into the area to re-organise the Dutch Fifth Column who had been forced underground after our great victory.' Pointing at me with the ruler, he continued, 'You are one of those spies, aren't you? Hiding behind a pack of lies! Don't think that just because you are wearing a uniform, you are safe. You are still a filthy spy and will be punished as such unless of course, you can show me otherwise.'

'How can I show you otherwise when I have already told you the truth?' I protested.

'How dare you shout at me,' he yelled. 'Didn't I tell you to address me as *Herr* Major? We will check your story and if you are telling lies, God help you! In the meantime you will be kept in solitary confinement to remember the truth. Tomorrow, I want to know . . . where you landed . . . where you have been . . . and the names of the people you contacted. Now get out!' He called the guard who escorted me back to Cell A8.

Shaken and desperately worried, I sat on my bed for a while with my head in my hands. I realised that, somehow, I had to stick to my story and prayed that the army were far too busy to report on the circumstances of my capture. As if to imprint it on my mind, I repeated the answers over and over again. I didn't sleep that night and approached the next day with a fearful apprehension but, to my amazement, nothing happened. No-one came near me, the guards looked away whenever I addressed them and the absolute silence of my surroundings became oppressive. The days seemed endless and the continuous anxiety of awaiting a further grilling really got me down until I realised that this was a ploy to break my spirit.

'Well,' I thought, 'I am damned if I am going to let the swine beat me, so I have got to find something to occupy my mind.' As often happens, good fortune came to my aid. In the pleat of my field dressing pocket I had at some time slipped the stub of a pencil only two inches long which, by good luck, had missed the search. This dirty little bit of wood was to become invaluable to me because with it, I was able to create a very rough pack of cards which gave me hours of pleasure.

I had previously noticed that the German 'loo' paper was kept in open wooden boxes nailed to the door jambs between the pans. It was thick and coarse and supplied in cut squares rather than in rolls. Pretending to be suffering from diarrhoea, I persuaded the guard to take me to the lavatory every four hours and on each occasion, collected extra 'bumph' which I concealed under my shirt. By halving the sheets, I soon had sufficient to inscribe a full pack and with it was able to defeat the solitude of my confinement. From then onwards, my day between meals was split up into a routine consisting of exercises, mental contemplation and prayer and innumerable practice hands of bridge.

During the many days that followed, I didn't see a soul but was subjected to various discomforts, such as leaving the light on all night, turning the heat on full blast with the shutters closed, or failing to respond to a 'loo call'. It didn't worry me unduly although I resented being unwashed and unshaven.

In my periods of contemplation I became conscious that, unwillingly, I was temporarily out of the battle and wondered how my old associates were faring. One day, I composed a poem expressing this thought:

For all my comrades in the fight tonight,
    Out there amidst the storm and tempestry,
I breathe a soldier's prayer, begrudging me
    This simple cell, where there's so little light.

Throughout the battle, I was truly blessed
    With precious life. For though my door is barred
My bed is paradise and yet I'm sleeping hard
    Well knowing that I strive not with the rest.

Safe as a prisoner, I cannot now complain,
    For here I'm sheltered from the stormy spaces
But there are some tonight who face the rain
    And some who'll never feel it on their faces.

Oh what's the use of shelter overhead,
If in my heart, I feel the rain instead.

Change in Tactics

Despite my rankling at being a prisoner, I derived personal satisfaction
that I had 'mentally' beaten the Germans, who presumably assumed
that the hours of solitary would soften me up. So when on 5 November,
nearly a month later, my door was opened and I was told to follow, I
approached my second interrogation with braver spirit. As it turned
out, it was not to be the *Gestapo* again but a youngish looking
Intelligence Officer of the *Luftwaffe* whose approach was so completely
different that, initially, I was tempted to be receptive.

'Ah, Captain Morrison, I am *Hauptmann* Muller. Sorry that you have
been kept waiting so long for our talk, but I have been away. Anyway,
won't you sit down . . . have a cigarette. You don't smoke? I wish I
didn't. Before the war I was a cabin steward with our national airline
and, because we could buy them so cheaply, I developed this bad
habit. Fortunately, my job also improved my languages and so I am
now used as an interrogator – somewhat safer than a Glider Pilot, I'm
sure!'

'Now,' he continued. 'According to these notes, you state that you
took part in the Arnhem landings, but the Major who first interrogated
you has suggested that you may be a contact man with the Dutch underground. My job is to examine every part of your story and therefore
you must just tell me all about your experiences, from start to finish. I
would like to know details of the places and the people that you saw
because, quite honestly, unless you can satisfy me that you are not such

a person, I will have no alternative but to hand you back to the *Gestapo*. I am sure that you understand my problem, so please help me to help you!' With that, he leaned back and put his feet on the table.

'Shall we start at the beginning. You are a Captain in the Glider Pilot Regiment. At which airfield were you based?'

'Here we go,' I thought, 'first the softening up, next the veiled threat.'

'You must know *Hauptmann* that I cannot answer that,' I replied quietly, 'but for what it is worth, I shall repeat the events from my capture until arriving at *Stalag* 12A.' Without giving him the chance to pursue his original line of questioning, I launched forth into a lengthy tirade at the inhuman treatment we had received on the long journey. I described in detail the filthy conditions in our carriage and the fact that the guards, whilst finding food for themselves, only gave scraps of bread to their hungry prisoners. My vehement exposition on the treatment of captured aircrew seemed to do the trick, for my interrogator listened for a while and then, obviously realising that I was warming up to the subject, looked at his watch and held up his hand.

'Yes, yes Captain, I am sorry that you were in the hands of the Army, who may be excellent soldiers but are often poor administrators. Now let's get back to your story.'

For the next hour, he talked around the Arnhem battle, shooting the unexpected question about my regiment and of the troops that we carried. I adopted a standard reply: 'You must know that I cannot tell you that.' Finally, in rather bad grace, he dismissed me with a curt, 'OK we shall continue tomorrow, when I hope you will be more co-operative.' During the next two days he continued to examine my story, trying to trip me up on detail and interspersing the conversation with questions about the tugs and the squadrons that we flew behind, but once more without any beneficial result.

He even produced a large photograph of a Horsa glider and queried the English name of the various sections. 'What are these "pieces" below the wings?' he would ask as if it was some secret weapon. 'What is their purpose?'

'They are exactly what you have on your bombers, FLAPS, but in action we don't trouble to lift them back as the glider will not be going anywhere after landing!' I replied with a grin.

Thus it continued, question after question, until having satisfied himself that I knew something about the aircraft that I claimed to fly, he seemed to accept my whole story. Then suddenly, he switched to asking my opinion on the morale of the British public now they were being subjected to bombardments by the V1 and V2 rockets.

For a while I remained silent, not knowing how best to answer and then resolved to fall back on the old trick of replying with another question.

90

'It would be silly of me to pretend that people don't mind, of course they do, but let me ask how your own family, sitting in the damp and discomfort of bomb shelters, would react knowing that the end of the war is in sight? Personally, I sincerely believe that your Government have underestimated the spirit of the British people. This indiscriminate bombing by pilotless aircraft has in fact, lifted the morale to even greater heights and where before, there might have been those who deplored our slaughter of women and children, the nation is now demanding a full and savage retribution.'

For a moment I felt that perhaps I had gone too far, but then, with a smirk, he concluded our interview. 'Let me assure you Captain Morrison, you are far safer as a prisoner-of-war in Germany. The V1 and V2 are only the first of a series of horrific weapons that we will unleash shortly. Then we will see who is winning the war and how the so-called spirit of the British will stand up to real destruction. You can go back to your cell.'

On my return, I gave thought to the conversation. I realised that the Germans must now be getting desperate and that Hitler's thugs could resort to the ultimate weapons of gas and germ warfare. The havoc that would be caused if they dropped bacterial bombs into the main London reservoirs when thousands of innocent people would die before the authorities could do anything about it, was too terrible to contemplate. I wondered how my own family would fare in these circumstances for we lived at the coast and in the direct line of attack on Portsmouth. Then, putting myself in *Hauptmann* Muller's shoes, I realised that he had received a pretty straight rebuff from me, and that it was only human nature for him to take me down a peg or two.

The next day saw a decided change in treatment. My boots were returned to me and I was escorted to a wash room where soap and a safety razor were supplied. What joy to be fresh and clean once more and, whilst the scraping off of a month's old beard was hard work, the effect of that shave did wonders to my morale.

At about 10 o'clock, I was ushered into the interrogation room but, on this occasion, Muller greeted me with a broad smile.

'Your questioning is over Captain, and you will leave for a PoW camp this afternoon. I have enjoyed our discussion and am satisfied that you are the Glider Pilot that you claim to be. In fact, I have known all about you for days! You command No 5 Flight and you normally fly behind a squadron of Stirlings. You took part in the D-Day landings with success and at Arnhem, you flew in the Anti-tank Battery.'

Noticing my discomfort, he added, 'Take pride in the fact that, despite harassment, you told us nothing, but there were others who were not so careful. Anyway, good luck and good bye. For you at least, the war is over!' Then, with a wave, he left the room.

For a while I remained standing there, grateful at having apparently weathered a traumatic experience and pondering over his final remark, 'For you the war is over'. This was the second time that I had been given this comment, but somehow, in my heart, I was not prepared to accept the situation. My thoughts were interrupted by the arrival of the guard who first took me back to A8 to collect the balance of my things including the brown envelope containing the personal items that had been taken from me at the search.

I was then escorted to the courtyard where, for the first time for what had seemed eternity, I could look up and see the bright sun shining on fleecy white clouds. Oh my, it was wonderful to be alive! My feelings were shared by the 34 aircrew who milled around the yard excitedly meeting old friends whom they had believed to be dead. There were men from both bomber and fighter squadrons, although, most of them had only been there a few days and none had received the 'full' workout given to me.

TEN

PRISONER-OF-WAR

En Route to Camp

After a while we were lined up, recorded and counted no less than three times, before being handed over to an NCO and guards under whose supervision we were embussed in two enclosed vans and taken to the Wetzlar 'Dulag'. This appeared to be a transit camp for aircrew and provided food and temporary accommodation. As far as I was concerned, its true merit was that it offered me the opportunity of filling in a Red Cross card which, by crossing out alternate words, would inform my beloved wife that, 'I was a prisoner/I was well/I was not injured'. I understand that this information was subsequently used by Lord Haw-Haw in one of his propaganda broadcasts from Germany, which were designed to capture the attention of the worried wives and parents whose husbands or sons had been posted as missing.

Arnhem had been such a disaster that, in the Glider Pilot Regiment alone, there were literally hundreds of pilots about whom there was no information. Indeed, when my wife telephoned the main Depot, they could only give her the scanty news that I had landed safely, but that later, I had been involved in some action from which I had not returned. However, as I had not been reported as 'killed', there was always the hope that I had been taken prisoner. It must have been a terrible time for her and I can imagine the wonderful relief she experienced when some kind person, in tuning her radio, recognised 'Haw-Haw's' twang, heard my name and address, and immediately telephoned her.

I was studiously writing out this card when I became aware of a large khaki figure standing by my side and glancing up I looked into the grinning countenance of Raith (Bill) Sykes, my second-in-command of No 5 Flight. Jumping up, we hugged each other with joy and performed a happy fandango much to the amusement of those present.

'Bill. God I'm glad to see you. Where have you been all my life?'

'Looking around for you, you old bastard,' he replied. 'Where the hell did you get to?' We promptly sat down and recounted our respective experiences.

'I was not as lucky as you with my family,' Bill said, 'after the second day, Mr and Mrs de Vos, the couple looking after Sgt Thomkins and myself, received the bad news that his brother had been picked up and handed over to the *Gestapo*, leaving the young wife and baby stranded. Understandably, Mrs de Vos felt that she should go over to help and, in the light of the circumstances, her husband wished to accompany her.

'They were obviously so worried that I insisted that they should leave, explaining that it would only be a matter of a few days before the British broke through. Unfortunately, we were arrested the next day whilst scrounging for food and kept in the local police cells for a week prior to being transported here. Sgt Thomkins has already been posted to a camp somewhere but I have been kept back pending collection of sufficient numbers. It is not too bad here, except it is desperately boring with so little to occupy you.'

For me, life suddenly took on a new meaning. Here was one of my closest friends with whom I was to share so much over the coming months and, during moments of depression, we would laugh about the happy times that we had had in the Flight and make plans for our own survival.

From Wetzlar, we took off to march to the railway siding where the old barred carriage awaited us. On this occasion we were each issued with a loaf of black rye bread, a chunk of cheese and a long sausage, with the news that it was to last us for a three day journey. In fact, the trip took on the same character as the earlier one with stops, starts and long waits at sidings and we were on board for seven days. In fairness to our guards, they managed to obtain some vegetable soup at three of the stations which certainly helped as it was beginning to get cold at night. In our compartment, apart from Bill, there were six RAF pilots and my 'pack of cards' was certainly well employed.

Finally, on 19 November, two months after Arnhem, our train steamed into the station at Barth, a town situated right up north on the Baltic coast. There we were handed over to our new guards, counted and marched under escort to *Stalag Luft* 1.

Upon reflection, I am sure that, during my early travels, I became so completely pre-occupied with personal survival that I lived only for the moment, and subconsciously avoided contemplating the future. I was safe and well and in any case the discomfort of capture was only temporary as the war would soon be over. Thank goodness this complacency was short-lived, for on that very journey from Barth station, when we were herded along like sheep, shouted at and prodded by the bullying guards, I regained my personal pride.

'Who are these scruffy oafs who are pushing us around?' I thought and took a closer look at them. Most were very third grade soldiers and, with the possible exception of the NCOs, would not normally be considered for combat duty. There they were, shuffling along, wearing balaclavas under their helmets to keep out the cold and in shapeless oversize greatcoats that reached right down to the ground. They looked like 'zombies' and I regarded them with contempt.

'What a rabble,' I thought, 'if these are examples of the "master race", just give me a chance to sort them out.' Little did I realise that in six months time, that wish would come true.

Stalag Luft 1

After about a half hours march, we passed what appeared to be a large 4 storey military barracks, and beyond could see the formidable triple line of wire fortifications with postern towers every 159 yards that surrounded the prisoner-of-war camp. As we reached the main gates with the emblem of the German eagle over its arch, more German soldiers ran out to march on either side, escorting us into a small compound where we halted outside an office block.

Once again we were lined up and counted by a Warrant Officer who, when satisfied that all were present, duly reported to the Camp Commandant who by now had come out onto a verandah accompanied by his Adjutant and two senior Allied officers. The party then walked down the ranks and inspected us, before returning to the verandah from which we were addressed.

First, the Camp Commandant, a smartly dressed army officer of about 60 years of age spoke to us in a cultured English voice.

> 'I am the Camp Commandant of *Stalag Luft* 1. A prisoner-of-war camp for captured airforce officers. The camp itself consists of three main compounds, and at present, houses 3000 American and 1600 Commonwealth aircrews. I mention these figures so that you will understand that, with these large numbers, discipline and good behaviour are essential for the well-being of the whole community.
>
> 'It follows that you will be expected to comply with the rules and regulations laid down and any officer failing to do so will be disciplined. Similarly, attempts to escape will be dealt with most seriously and my guards have instructions to shoot any person crossing the warning wire of the perimeter fence or found outside your quarters when you are confined to them.
>
> 'As Commandant, I am prepared to co-operate fully with the two senior officers here, Col Goodyear and Group Captain Ward, in the smooth running of the camp and for the general benefit of all prisoners. However, if there is improper conduct or insubordination of any kind,

not only will the culprits themselves be severely punished but the privileges and concessions, such as food parcels, for the whole camp will be withdrawn.

'At first you will find it difficult to adapt yourselves to the restrictions but you must realise that you are now prisoners and non-combatants and will remain as such until the end of the war. Therefore accept and make the best of your changed circumstances and strive to become a worthy member of your community. I now hand you over to the senior Allied Officers.'

With that, he saluted and marched back into the office block.

Col Goodyear then took over to address us in a broad American accent:

'I guess that it is inopportune to welcome you to *Stalag Luft* 1, but I greet you as a fellow prisoner and wish you well. Today will be spent in allocating your accommodation and kitting you out. Then, once you have settled in, Group Captain Ward will interview the Commonwealth officers whilst I will see the Americans, not only to discuss any problems that you may have but also to explain the camp rules in detail. The Camp Adjutant will now call the roll and read out your Block and room number.'

At this stage an elderly *Luftwaffe* Officer stepped forward and holding a board in front of him, called out our names. Upon receiving the answer 'here' he would nominate the Block and room number. Mine was Block 10 room 9 and, to my delight, Bill's was the same. That complete, we were split into groups under the supervision of a guard to visit the stores for the issue of a cake of blue soap, shaving brush, razor and towel after which, we made our way to the Ablutions Block where we were greeted by a cheerful American medical orderly.

'Welcome to my kingdom, buddies. I guess this is going to be the finest thing that will happen to you today – a good shit, shower and shave! But first I have to examine everyone just in case you have been unfortunate enough to pick up German fleas or ticks on your journey – believe me they are real bad.'

The hot shower was heavenly and, after a good shave, I really felt that I could face up to the confines of prison life, but I was soon to be disillusioned. My next move was to what I assume was the Records Office, where the pushing and shoving started up once more. This time it was an arrogant little German Corporal who grabbed me roughly by the arm and propelled me into a cubicle. He then proceeded to thrust a form into my hand on which I had to inscribe my army number, rank and name. This information was then transferred onto a slate which was hung around my neck whilst I was photographed like a criminal. Then, to add to my ignominy, he looked for birth marks and finding none, promptly grabbed my thumb to ram it onto an ink pad prior to forcing it down on a card. By this time, I was getting very cross as the record card I finally recovered clearly shows, and had it not been for the restraining word from Bill, I might well have clocked him one.

As we passed from building to building, we caught sight of the main Commonwealth Compound where 50 or 60 'kriegies' were lining the wire to see if any members of their own squadron were the new arrivals. Bill noticed a couple of Glider Pilots who waved madly and shouted advice which we couldn't hear anyway.

My last visit was to the Group Captain's room which was in the Senior Officers' Block. Apart from the bunk beds, it was equipped with a stove, a couple of cupboards and a table behind which were seated two officers. The first was the Group Captain whom we had seen at the reception. He was of average height and build, and had a cheerful smile and happy disposition. In contrast, the second was considerably larger, with a ruddy face which seemed to carry a permanent scowl. He was the Camp Liaison Officer and looked a pretty tough character which aspect was certainly portrayed during our subsequent conversation.

As I entered, Ward rose to his feet and held out his hand with a warm greeting:

'Ah, Captain Morrison, please sit down and have a cup of tea. First let me introduce ourselves, I am the senior Commonwealth officer and Bob Bone here is my deputy. I served in Bomber Command and was shot down early in the war. In fact, I have been a prisoner for 4 years so, by now, I am fairly used to it. Bob was a fighter pilot and in keeping with that breed, considers himself superior! Mind you we haven't rated him against Glider Pilots yet because you are the first Army flyers that we have had here.' At which Bone snorted and waved a hand in my direction.

'Now,' continued Ward, 'gliders weren't in service when I did my flying and as I have to get to know you fellows, would you be kind enough to tell me how you became one.'

'Perhaps I should first explain,' I said. 'We are soldiers who volunteered to join the Regiment. Initially I was interviewed by a selection committee and when approved, posted to the main Depot where for the next two months, we were subjected to a pretty rigorous battle course. This had two objectives, the first was to weed out those who were unfit or did not have the necessary 'guts' and the second was to keep us busy until flying facilities were available. Having weathered the physical hammering, I was then sent to an RAF station for the standard Elementary Flying Training which I passed satisfactorily. My next move was to learn to fly light gliders and finally I was transferred to a

Heavy Glider course which, when completed, rated me as an "operational Glider Pilot" and I was posted to a Squadron.'

'Very interesting,' commented Ward. 'But what gliders did you fly? How big are they by comparison with the towing aircraft? And who did you carry?'

I thought for a moment, 'What is he really after?' and answered very generally.

'Well sir, I flew the Horsa which has a similar wingspan to a bomber and on D-Day carried men into Normandy, whilst at Arnhem, I took a loaded jeep, anti-tank gun and crew.'

'A loaded jeep and gun,' interrupted Bone.' That sounds heavy so I suppose that you were towed by a powerful aircraft from one of the bomber squadrons. If you give me the number, I will check if we have any of their pilots here.'

'Yes, you are right,' I replied.

'What the hell do you mean. Yes you are right,' stormed Bone.

'I was confirming your statement. We were towed by powerful aircraft.'

'Look here Morrison, I asked you a civil question and try to make you feel at home, and all I get is a stupid answer.'

For a moment there was silence. Then looking straight at Ward, I spoke slowly.

'I am sorry sir, I don't mean to be rude, but I have already had a tough time of interrogation by the *Gestapo* followed by a month in solitary, and I would ask if you will excuse me answering questions until I know who to trust.'

At this they both burst out laughing. 'Well done young Morrison,' chortled Bone, now smiling, 'The Goons have their stooges and you can never be too careful. To be quite honest, we also have to be sure that you are not a plant.'

'Ask any Glider Pilot,' I replied.

'Well for my own interest, I would like to hear all about the battle of Arnhem because we are inclined to be brainwashed here,' commented Ward. 'So, when you are satisfied with me, perhaps we can have a chinwag about your experience. Now first let me tell you something about this camp and the sort of life we live here. *Stalag Luft* 1 is well established as camps go and in total we have about 4600 aircrew officers here. The Camp Commandant and most of his men are strict but fair and provided we don't cause trouble, we are not buggered about too much. There are exceptions of course and over a period of time, you will get to know the bad tempered and mean guards. I realise that it is human nature to rebel against some of the petty restrictions that we receive, but take my advice and play it cool.

'Similarly, amongst your future associates you may find those who are difficult and downright rude but please remember that some of the chaps have been prisoners from the early days of the war and they tend to resent newcomers who may attract attention when they bring news from "home".'

He paused for a moment then, lowering his voice, he continued. 'In due course Captain you will learn a good deal more about the "internal organisation", suffice to say, we have ways and means of securing equipment which is invaluable to maintain contact with the responsible section in British Intelligence. This is achieved through the Equipment Officer who has certain guards in his pocket and with whom he maintains a barter system using the "goodies" that we receive. It is important therefore that others do not try to trade with the Germans, otherwise they will queer the market. Now, I require from you a solemn undertaking that anything you learn about our organisation will be kept secret and not discussed with anyone, but anyone. Do I have your promise? Good.

'Finally, following the execution by the German High Command of a number of escapees from a *Stalag Luft* camp and also the incident of chaining prisoners, I, in conjunction with Col Goodyear, have decided to withdraw, temporarily, the basic edict that it is the duty of an officer to try to escape. Accordingly, the "escape committee" will cease to operate and all prisoners are advised, not ordered, that it would be wiser to await liberation rather than to attempt to break out at this stage. I fully realise Captain, that with your military background and the inborne aggression of an airborne soldier, you may resent this guidance but take my assurance that we already have emergency plans for this camp and I don't want anyone to jeopardise them by ill-conceived attempts at escape. Do you have any comment?'

'Yes sir, whilst I understand and will obey your instructions, it rankles me to have been taken prisoner and I have not finished with this bunch yet, so if I can help in any way, please count me in.'

'Well, we will have to think about that Captain. In the meantime, be patient and make good friends with your fellow "kriegies". Good luck and if at any time you wish to see me, my door is always open.'

I left his room feeling happier that all was not lost, in that there was some organisation through which to continue the fight. Little did I then realise its extent nor that there were already facilities for communicating with England. Contacts with outside workmen enabled us to send regular reports and our 'ground-to-air' signals were picked up by high flying aircraft and photographed. Through the Intelligence Officer, we received daily a typed précis of the BBC news which we were able to compare with the English edition of the German news circulated by the Camp Commandant. Indeed, I was soon to learn just how efficient our lines of communication were – but more of that later.

My immediate problem was to find Bill Sykes and to report to the officer in charge of number 10 Block. I located him by the entrance to the compound, talking to Glider Pilots of other squadrons who quickly took us in hand and escorted us to our new home. This consisted of one of a total of 14 identical long wooden single-storey huts, which stood on brick piers about two foot high. Running down the centre was a passageway with doors leading off on either side into the barrack rooms. At one end was the OCs room, which he shared with his Adjutant, whilst at the main entrance end, there was an area which housed a cast-iron coal stove with four hotplates and a small oven.

The Officer in charge of Number 10 Block was Squadron Leader Wilson, who kindly met us and after a quick briefing, took us round to each room and introduced us to the 16 occupants. Understandably, the first thing that they wanted to talk about was the conditions at home and how the British people were standing up to the onslaught of V2 rockets. From the German news they had heard horrific stories of the devastation caused by this weapon and they were much relieved to be told that the actual casualties were small when compared with a heavy bombing raid.

Finally, Bill and I were taken to Room 9 where we were to meet a wonderful bunch of fellows who immediately took us to their hearts and made us feel welcome. There was a complete cross-section of bomber and fighter crews, hailing from Britain, Canada, Australia, New Zealand, Rhodesia and South Africa and, being such a mixed group, I would spend hours with them talking about their lives before the war and the politics of their countries.

Much has been written about life in prison camps, of the boredom and frustration, of inactivity, the lack of food and the mean and vindictive attitude of some of the guards – known to me now as 'Goons'. As far as I was concerned, I soon recognised that there was a danger of becoming lethargic and passively accepting captivity. Many of the PoWs had become 'sack hounds' in that, once roll call was over, they would retire to their bunk to read until the next meal time. This attitude was alien to my thinking, and I promptly set about planning a programme of physical and mental activity which not only kept me fit but uplifted my resolve to be 100% ready when the time of trial arrived. Apart from a morning and afternoon constitutional walk round the perimeter track with Bill, I was fortunate in that, being a keen sportsman, I was able to join in every game going and played soccer for Scotland and rugby for England against the Rest.

On the intellectual side, I decided to learn a language and joined a brother Glider Pilot in the study of Norwegian under the tuition of a pilot from that country, in exchange for improving his English. My friend, Bruce Winter, wanted to learn because he was engaged to a

Norwegian girl, whilst I thought it might be useful because, if escape came, it would probably be via the Baltic. In any event, it would be a good part of the world to visit after the war.

During the early days at the camp, I met up with Col McNeill (Mac), who had commanded one of the Airlanding Battalions with great valour at Arnhem. He was later to establish our own little fighting unit, named the Field Force and asked me to serve as his Adjutant. Indeed, it was on his recommendation that I was subsequently taken into the inner circle of the camp's undercover activities and was soon to be involved in the collation of strategic information for MI6.

I Spy

It all started one morning when Mac collected me to join him and Group Captain Ward on a stroll round the perimeter wire.

'Well young Morrison, how are you settling down?' asked Ward.

'Fine sir. I have a great bunch of chaps in my room who have been most kind and helpful,' I replied.

'Good. Now during our little talk, you mentioned that you would like to help. Are you still keen? All right, then here's a job for you. I want you to prepare a detailed report and sketch not only of the German defences around the camp but also of the probable fortifications within an area of say a couple of miles of us.'

When he saw my puzzled expression on the latter requirement, he grinned.

'What you don't know yet is that you have been appointed "messenger boy" for Camp Management. You will be supplied with an American uniform and given a pass enabling you to visit each of the compounds. On most days you will be required to contact people in the American areas and thus will ultimately become acquainted with the whole of *Stalag Luft* 1. It will then be a simple matter to walk right round the perimeter wire and record the position of weapon pits etc.'

'That's great sir,' was my excited comment. 'I will be happy to do the job, but you mentioned a couple of miles. Does this mean that I am to join a working party?'

'No,' answered Ward. 'That is another plan that I have in store for you. As you will know, an American Officer was shot and killed last night. He was playing poker with some friends in another block when the air-raid siren sounded and all the windows had to be shuttered. Sadly, instead of heading straight back to his own room in an adjacent Block, he decided to stay for a while. However as the raid continued for quite a time, he foolishly opted to make a dash for it and one of the guards, seeing him, shot him down. Needless to say, a serious complaint has already been lodged with the Camp Commandant but whilst he expressed sympathy, he firmly maintained that the guard was acting strictly in accordance with instructions and in fact the officer concerned had contravened standing orders. However, as a concession, he has agreed to allow his room-mates to attend the funeral at the Barth Cemetery.

'The funeral will take place the day after tomorrow and you will be one of the party. If you are happy, I want you to come back with me now to meet Col Goodyear's second-in-command and he will kit you out and arrange for you to meet this chap's friends.'

Thus it was that, after roll call the following morning, I was escorted over to the American compound and introduced to the dead pilot's room-mates. I can only presume that they had been briefed about my task because they accepted me quite happily and I spent a very enjoyable time with them, listening to their adventures. Then the next day, we met up again at the main gate to assemble behind the horse-drawn hearse carrying the coffin. In due course, the padre arrived with four guards and we set forth to the cemetery.

By arrangement, I positioned myself in the centre of the group frantically looking in all directions until we finally reached the graveyard. When we arrived at the side of the grave, four of his friends lifted the coffin and lowered it safely, after which the padre held a short burial service that ended with each of us saluting our departed associate. The guards who had accompanied us stood silently some 20 yards away but, even at that distance, must have sensed the hatred expressed in the attitude of the American pilots, because they suddenly became watchful and apprehensive. After we had each dropped earth on the coffin, the mood eased somewhat and we finally lined up once more to make our way back.

Our route took us past a large military barracks which turned out to be an Anti-aircraft Training School where there were a number of light and heavy flak gun emplacements. These were supported by weapon pits with all-round fields of fire, and in the centre there were some small semi-sunken buildings which could have well been used as control centres or to store ammunition or pyrotechnics.

Carefully, I calculated the various distances and memorised as much as possible and, on my return to camp, I immediately prepared my preliminary sketch map. During the following week I walked all round the camp itself, making notes of the dug trenches outside the wire and also the exact position of the postern towers. Then, when satisfied, I prepared my final report and handed it into Bob Bone.

How this information was submitted to England I shall never know, but the wonderful proof of my efforts was revealed to me when I visited our Regimental Headquarters after VE-Day, for there was a large aerial photograph of our camp on which had been superimposed the very information that I had supplied. In April 1945, this very document had been issued to units of the Airborne Division, for it was then quite on the cards that it might be necessary to launch an attack on Barth to rescue the prisoners. This was my first realisation of how well *Stalag Luft* 1 was in touch with the UK and specifically, how a prisoner can still contribute towards the war effort.

ELEVEN

PREPARATION FOR REVOLT

Reconnaissance

After my initial introduction into the undercover activities of the camp, things went quiet for a while, until one afternoon, Col McNeill came over to our block.

'Hello John. Are you feeling energetic? Good, well what about a stroll around the compound?'

'OK Mac, give me a minute to finish peeling the spuds. I am cook tonight.'

Having cleaned up, we set off and once we were clear of the other groups, he turned to me and said:

'Well John, your report is on its way and the "powers that be" seem very pleased with it. Well done. We now have a far more important task. As you will have heard on our English news, the Germans have been moving some of the prisoner-of-war camps right down into central Austria and the wretched "kriegies" have been forced to march for days on end without food and water. The reason given, is that the re-location of prisoners away from the possible battle area is in their own interests, but we believe that Hitler is planning to use them as hostages. Now, with the advance of the Russians along the Baltic from the East and the Allies from the West, *Stalag Luft* 1 could well be the next camp to be moved and the senior officers here are determined that we will "sit tight" and refuse to leave our shelter and supplies of food. Therefore, when the time comes, we will rise up and revolt to take over the camp which we will hold until help arrives.'

'That sounds all very fine,' I interjected. 'But how the hell do we over-throw the German guards? And with what?'

'That John, is the very plan that you and I have to prepare. The joint senior officers would like to have some ideas on how this could possibly be achieved and we have a week to make suggestions. So I reckon that we should both study the problem and meet every afternoon to air our thoughts. As a start, I believe that we should know what we are up against and should establish the number of guards, their weapons and the possible reinforcements that they might obtain from the Flak

School. I will speak to the "contact man" and see if he can gather this information from a co-operative guard. In the meantime would you have a good look at the postern towers around the perimeter and see how we could isolate them.'

Sensing my incredulous reaction, he continued. 'I realise old chap, that this is a tall order but the problem could well arise and we must be prepared. Anyway good luck with your personal "think tank". See you tomorrow afternoon.'

So it was that I gathered further details of the camp defences and assessed in my own mind the task that confronted us. Then a couple of days later I gave my initial report.

'Mac, looking first at the German positions, it is abundantly clear that they have placed considerable reliance on the towers which dominate the surrounding fence. These boxlike platforms stand 20 feet above the ground and in each there is a light machine-gun mounted on a tripod to provide an all-round field of fire.

'Alongside this weapon there is a moveable searchlight which, during previous alarms could be seen to illuminate brightly the line of the wire and the general area of the compound. In our section of the camp alone there are six of these towers located 150 yards apart and, during the day, they are each manned by a single guard with a second after dusk. The rest of the defence system seems to be directed against possible attacks from outside because the guards have dug two-man weapon pits in the area of their quarters facing away from the wire.'

'That's good John and what are your thoughts on how we can neutralise the towers?'

'Well I must confess that my initial assessment of our chances is pretty dismal. Quite obviously Mac, a frontal attack across the compound, over or through two lines of 9-foot-high wire and up 20 steps to reach the machine-gun would be suicidal. The towers are inter-supporting in that men attacking tower number 3 would also come under fire from those on either side. Furthermore, the machine-gunners, in their panic, might direct fire into the prisoners' rooms and the subsequent carnage would be disastrous.'

'I never thought that this would be an easy one,' commented Mac. 'I have not yet heard from our "contact man" but I should have the required details tomorrow. In the meanwhile, don't worry, I am sure that one of us will hit on a solution.'

Quite honestly, at first the whole concept looked impossible and for hours I trudged round the wire trying in vain to puzzle out a plan. At night, I would lie awake on my 'sack' pondering over even the most far fetched ideas. Could we construct an armoured wagon of the laundry cart with which to ram the wire? Could we burrow underneath a tower? Could we capture the Camp Commandant with his senior staff at the next major meeting and hold them hostage against surrender of the guards? So it went on until, one evening it occurred to me to put myself in the position of a guard. What would I fear most during a possible attack? The answer was darkness! Therefore the lights would have to be our number one objective.

I could not wait for the following afternoon but contacted Mac immediately for our walk.

'I think I've got it,' I cheerfully declared. 'The thing that our guards would fear most is a black-out and therefore our plan must be based on a night attack in which the searchlights will first be rendered useless. In this situation, the gunners would no longer be self-supporting and they would be reluctant to fire along fixed lines down the wire for fear of hitting their own men. Furthermore, if we could add to the confusion by generating masses of smoke, it might be possible to assault the towers with success, especially if we could also devise some means of setting the woodwork alight.'

'OK,' Mac commented. 'Perhaps I can find out where the main sub-station is and if there is an emergency power plant. Now John, whilst you have been developing the rudiments of a plan, I have not been idle. I have drawn up our strategy in three phases. First, we have to choose and train a suitable force and here we are lucky to have ten Glider Pilots to act as leaders and instructors. Next, we have to find arms and ammunition for them and on this, our Procurement Officer already has ideas. Finally, we must work out the finer details and establish a comprehensive plan of attack. In effect, this should be our initial recommendation to the Senior Allied Officers and once we have received their approval, we will set about the formation of a Field Force and the organisation necessary to equip it.

Birth of Field Force – Procurement of Weapons

So it transpired that, over the next few weeks, we created three platoons of potential soldiers who would be officered by Glider Pilots on the British side and by men who had had military training amongst the Americans.

As Adjutant, one of my duties was to teach elementary tactics, which was done under the guise of 'First Aid' lectures. In these, having first satisfied ourselves that no 'Goons' were snooping around, I would lay out a few bandages and then give instruction in the use of German weapons and the basic rudiments of both attack and defence. During one of these lectures the lookout at the door called out 'Goons up' whereupon we promptly set upon each other with bandages and when

the guards looked in through the window, they saw, to their amusement, a number of casualties suitably trussed up!

The procurement of arms proved easier than at first anticipated for
whilst the Allies were advancing on both fronts, the Russians were by
far the nearest and every German soldier who was fit was thrown into
the battle against them. Each day we would see the departure of the
younger guards who would be replaced by elderly men or Grade C
Militia and it was to the individuals who were posted to the Eastern
Front that our 'contact officer' made his approach.

'Can we have a chat,' he would say. 'From the news, it looks that the
Russians have broken through and are advancing fast along the Baltic
coast, whilst on the other flank, the British and Americans are pushing
eastwards. I understand that you have been posted to a regiment
opposing the Russians and despite your brave acceptance, it must be
a terrible prospect to be sent into battle against hundreds of tanks with
so little to fight them with! What ever will you do if you are over-run?
It's no use surrendering to the Bolshies – you know that they have no
time for prisoners. I am not saying that they shoot them but from what
I hear, they are herded into fields with no shelter and little food and
those who are still alive are marched off to labour camps. What a
ghastly prospect!'

Undoubtedly the guard felt the same way but usually mumbled
something like, 'Obviously, I'm not happy about the posting, but it is
just one of those things.'

'Please understand that I am not suggesting that you should be
disloyal,' would comment our man. 'But do you know what I would do
if I was in your shoes? When I left the camp, I would report to one of
the regiments on the Western Front and then, if over-run, I would join
the hundreds of German soldiers already giving themselves up to the
British. At least you would save yourself terrible suffering and, once a
prisoner, you would at least be dealt with decently and in accordance
with the Geneva Convention. By the way, are you married? Yes, then
you should also think about your family . . . now, I am not supposed
to do this, but you chaps have been fair with us and, if you decide to
accept my advice, why don't you come and have a talk to me and I will
see if I can't give you a letter in English to the Commanding Officer of
the troops that capture you, stating that you have been a just and kind
guard who has co-operated with Allied airmen in captivity.'

In most cases, the wretched man, torn between duty, his own safety
and the future prospects for his family would approach the officer.

'What do I have to do to co-operate?' he would ask.

'Well you have a problem and so do we. With the possible arrival of
the Russians, we are going to be confronted by stray bands of un-
disciplined troops scavenging for food. We want to be able to defend

our supplies and for this we will need guns and ammunition. As you will no longer need your Schmieser, rather than throw it away, hand it over to me in exchange for your "passport" to freedom.'

This quiet approach paid off handsomely for nearly every guard was by then, apprehensive at the possibility of being captured by the Russians. Accordingly, their conscience willingly forgot the unfortunate loss of a weapon or a box of grenades when the prospect of seeing their family again could be assured. Thus in the weeks to follow, we collected sufficient arms and ammunition to equip at least one platoon and, in addition, by various barter deals, we gathered together a sizeable quantity of bottles, petrol and paraffin with which to produce 'Molotov Cocktails'. All this equipment was carefully split up and hidden away in previously prepared caches.

Master Plan for Revolt

By then, we had given greater thought to the assault on the towers and, in particular, to setting them alight. Here the Americans came up with the idea of lobbing 'Molotov Cocktail' bottles onto the platform under cover of smoke. These would burst into flames and incinerate the machine-gunners. Then once the towers were alight, they could be kept burning by further bottles, thus adding to the smoke.

The problem was the accuracy of the 'flame throwers', who would have to project the bottle some 40 to 50 yards. Once again, ingenuity came to the rescue and our German 'hosts' were introduced to a new game which consisted of pairs of men, each standing in a 4-foot circle some 60 yards apart, into which they had to throw a firewood log of the size and weight of a filled bottle. This they did with all the 'hubba-bubba' of professional baseball players and, after a few days of practice, our 'pitchers' became surprisingly accurate and could practically guarantee three out of five with many close failures, which in any case would burst and add to the conflagration.

To add further confidence to the tower assault plan, Mac came back joyfully and announced, 'I've got wonderful news! The Goons have made a serious error in siting the main camp sub-station within yards of the Senior Allied Officers' quarters and the Sick Bay and, you'll never believe it, the auxiliary lighting plant is in the same building! Furthermore, as it is all within the main perimeter wire, its internal protection is limited to a single wire fence. Boy oh boy, what a bonus.'

Excited with this piece of good news, we were able to develop our plan which was based on a platoon of the Field Force assembling overnight in the Senior Allied Officers' hut, from whence they would break through the internal fence of the central area and assault the

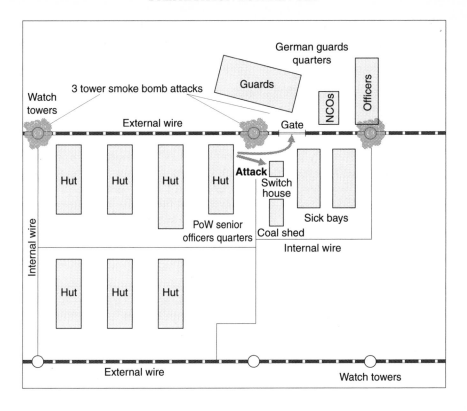

guards' sleeping quarters. At the same time, a section of men would capture the main electrical sub-station, together with the auxiliary lighting plant and put both out of commission.

Whilst this was proceeding, the occupants of the huts nearest the two towers overlooking the central area were to set them alight and burn bales of damp straw already stored under the floor. Once the smoke was thick enough, the 'Molotov' bottle throwers would then move into action to isolate these towers. The remainder of the Field Force would snipe at the rest of the towers and once automatic weapons were taken from the captured guards, would attack each of them in turn.

At last things seemed to be coming right and the once impossible task really looked feasible. We were now ready to rise up and were fully confident that we would have no problem in overwhelming our elderly guards, whose discipline was being eroded daily by bad news from both fronts.

Clearly, the whole issue that had prompted the plan in the first place was the threat of being forced to march southwards, and therefore it came as no surprise when at 5 o'clock on the afternoon of 29 April, the

109

German Camp commandant called the Senior Allied Officers into his office to announce that this would take place the following day. He came straight to the point:

> 'Gentlemen, I must inform you that today, I have been ordered to close this camp and to transfer all the prisoners to a location yet to be notified. This step has been necessary to safeguard your lives because, within one week, the town of Barth and the surrounding areas will become the centre of a bloody battle. I am conscious of the enormity of the task particularly as we will have to march *en masse* because there is no bulk transport available and the few trucks that I have been able to secure will have to be used to carry supplies of food. My staff is presently planning the route that we will have to take and the centres where meals will be provided and I will discuss these with you later. In the meantime, I am giving you 18 hours notice to prepare for the journey and I suggest . . .'

There was a sudden crash as Col Goodyear jumped up, knocking his chair backwards. Purple in the face he slammed his fist on the table and stood quivering with rage just two feet away from the Commandant.

'You bastards,' he shouted. 'You are flagrantly betraying the principles of the Red Cross Convention. How can your Command even think of moving nearly 5000 men away from their supplies of food with not the slightest prospect of anything to eat nor anywhere to sleep? It is a case of vicious mayhem perpetrated to kill off hundreds of innocent prisoners. You are criminals, making this move that will go down in history to the everlasting shame of the German people. I demand an immediate meeting with the Red Cross officials.'

'I am afraid that you are not in a position to demand anything,' responded the Commandant, now equally ruffled. 'My orders are to move and at noon tomorrow we march. Before your outburst, I was going to suggest that you distribute the stock of Red Cross parcels and instruct your men to wear warm clothing and carry a blanket for the journey.'

'Never,' yelled the Colonel. 'I accept that you have your orders, but I am about to issue mine . . . Not a single prisoner will move from this camp and we will resist you to the last man. I repeat, to the last man. We are staying here, so what is your attitude to that?'

For a moment the tension in the room was electric, but then the Commandant, looking down at his hands, quietly replied:

'You ask my attitude . . . my attitude is that I will not condone bloodshed in this camp. If you refuse to move, then I and my men will evacuate ourselves and leave you in sole control. However, let me make one thing quite clear, my responsibility is to protect these prisoners from being involved in the fighting. I have orders to march and I offer you safe conduct to another camp. If you reject my protection, then let it be on your head!'

'I will gladly accept the consequences,' replied Col Goodyear. 'But if we are now to protect ourselves, we must be armed. Quite obviously, when you depart, you will do so taking your personal weapons, so I would ask you to leave behind the rest.'

'All right. You must have something.' With a brief salute, the Commandant marched out of his office leaving the Senior Allied Officers in silence.

For a moment no-one moved and then Group Captain Ward, rising to his feet, clasped Goodyear by the shoulder and exclaimed, 'Wonderful, I am proud of you.'

'Thanks, but now we really have to get organised. Will you collect the team together in my room say at 8 o'clock so that we can run through our earlier plan for Operation *Freedom* and bring along some of your "hooch". I guess we need a little drink to prepare us for the future.'

Twelve

FREE

Operation *Freedom*

So it was that at 1 a.m. the next morning, Major Steinhauer reported that the German guards had evacuated the camp. To the bulk of the 'kriegies', this came as a complete surprise and they awoke to realise that there was no-one in the postern towers. Within minutes, the whole camp went wild with people rushing around in their 'long-johns' clapping each other on the back shouting with joy. 'We're free ... we're free.'

Then at 8 o'clock, Colonel Goodyear spoke on the public address system:

> 'Fellow "kriegies", yesterday afternoon, the German Camp Commandant told me that he had received orders to close the camp and to march all the prisoners here southwards into alternative accommodation. Indeed, he gave us 18 hours notice to be ready. I refused to obey his instructions saying that we were not prepared to move away from our supplies of food and shelter. After a heated argument, he capitulated stating that, as he was officially responsible for our protection, any rejection on our part, released him from this duty. Therefore, henceforth I would be accountable for the decision to stay. I gladly accepted that and early this morning the German guards marched off.
>
> 'Now, where do we stand? There is still a war on and we are in enemy territory, so we are not out of danger yet. However, I should tell you that for 3 months now, we have been preparing for this predicament and secretly, have been training a Field Force who will operate outside the camp to secure certain strategic objectives. They are now fully armed and will shortly commence their important duties. Similarly, we will have an Internal Group responsible for our security, because, with the worsening food situation locally, we can expect scavenging bands. For most of us here, I would ask you all to continue with your normal daily routine. Stay in the camp and enjoy the prospect that help will come soon. Good luck.'

As Adjutant of the Field Force, I had already made my way to Col McNeill's room and together we decided to site our Headquarters in the Camp office where we had the facilities of desks and telephones. During the early morning, the Platoon Commanders had collected their men and housed them in the barracks immediately behind our HQ. A thorough search of the guards' quarters brought to light a number of rifles, grenades and machine-guns and subsequently, we were able to supplement these from the Armourer's store which fortunately had been left unlocked. Hence, within hours of our take-over we had sufficient to equip the whole Field Force. A further useful find were some large scale maps of the area which enabled the 'escape committee' draftsmen to make sufficient copies for the Section leaders.

Whilst these preparations were in hand, Col McNeill was called to an urgent meeting of the 'Camp Management' in the Commandant's office and, when he arrived, Col Goodyear brought the group to order.

'Gentlemen, we have discussed in detail the various priorities necessary to implement our plan Operation *Freedom*. I have called Col McNeill here to receive instructions for the Field Force that he commands. Colonel, the committee of Senior Officers present have established four major tasks for the Field Force on which I now direct you:

1. You will locate and take over the previous sources of fresh food and vegetables to the camp. Lt James of our Commissariat, who previously liaised with the Germans on supplies, will accompany your men to the bakery and the market.
2. You will capture and hold our means of exodus – namely the *Luftwaffe* satellite airfield south of Barth and ensure that it is operational within four days for use by transport aircraft.
3. The "Internal Force" that you have now established will defend the camp against possible outside invasion by local refugees looking for food and shelter.
4. Finally, you will make contact with the Russians and advise them of our presence.

Any questions? Right then, I won't delay you further as you have much to achieve. Good luck.'

Upon return to our Headquarters, Mac sat down opposite me and grinned.

'It's good to be back in business again, isn't it? Now John, I want a while to plan how to achieve our objectives. What worries me is the lack of weapons for the Internal Force. We have machine-guns but they are still in the towers. Can you arrange for one of the Glider Pilot officers to resite them on the ground, and will you please have a look at the Flak School and see what they have there.'

Not knowing what I would meet in opposition, I collected a Section from one of the Platoons and we carefully made our way across to a large red brick building about 200 yards away. Fortunately for us, the school had been abandoned and everywhere there were signs of complete panic in flight. I suppose that the German staff had tried to destroy documents, for the contents of all the filing cabinets had been emptied into the centre of the rooms, but no-one had got around to burning the pile. We even found a safe that had been left open and a cash box with a little money in it. This was duly confiscated and later handed over to the Purchasing Officers.

Whilst in the building, we also examined the second and third floors where there were self-contained flats for the instructors. In retrospect, I really don't know what we were looking for, as all the able bodied men had departed, but what we found made me feel quite sick. Huddled in the inner rooms of most of the flats we would come across the pathetic remnants of a terrified family, consisting of perhaps a wife, beside herself with grief and anxiety, and a couple of small children grovelling under the bed. In some cases, the grandmother would be lying in the bed, shivering with fright in anticipation of the arrival of the Russians. Poor creatures, they had nowhere to go as, at that stage, there was no way of travelling home and, from rumours received, they understood that they could expect nothing but cruel and brutal treatment in the hands of the invaders.

As there did not seem to be any weapons in the main block, we extended our search into the out-buildings and came upon a hut which was locked and barred that looked interesting. A few minutes with a crowbar found in the garage and, hey-presto, there was the armoury with rifles and machine-guns neatly secured in racks along two walls, with boxes of ammunition on the floor. There was even a handcart which we quickly loaded up to take the arms back to the camp.

Other finds in the Flak School were a jeep-type pickup and a 3-ton truck which were both jacked up in the process of being serviced, together with a real bonus of a petrol bowser trailer which was half full. Leaving the two vehicles, we proudly pushed the bowser and handcart back to the camp to a rowdy chorus of 'Yo heave ho' and handed them over, prior to arranging for a couple of mechanics to get the rest of the vehicles mobile.

Ensuring Food Supplies

The first priority was to secure a continued supply of fresh food and No 1 Platoon, commanded by Glider Pilot Lt Bob Conchi, was given the task of doing this. Fortunately, some three months previously, the German Commandant, faced with the depletion of his own personnel, had brought in 20 American NCOs to act as working parties for the collection and distribution of bread and vegetables for the camp. They had operated under the supervision of Lt Jimmy James, having first been required to promise that they would not attempt to escape.

The camp already had supply contracts and Bob was required to ensure their continuance. He was well suited for this task, for he spoke German and had a fiery temperament that brooked no nonsense. His platoon was already fully equipped with rifles and three sub-machine-guns and, during the first afternoon of freedom, they had practised the basic rudiments of advancing in open order.

At 8 a.m. on 1 May, Bob and his men, accompanied by Jimmy James and a food party, sallied forth towards the bakery which was located in the outskirts of the town of Barth. Obviously, Jimmy James knew the way and led them through the back streets which were quite deserted both of vehicles and people. There were no soldiers nor policemen anywhere, and whilst the occupants of the houses could be seen peeking from behind curtained windows, not a soul attempted to stop them or even enquire where they were going.

'It was quite eerie,' commented Bob. 'Barth is a small town and yet it was completely empty. Obviously, the Germans were anticipating its occupation by the Russians and understandably, those who could flee had already done so, leaving behind the infirm, the sick and the elderly who had nowhere to go. Shops were closed and I began to wonder where the population bought supplies. Possibly they had stocked up but surely they still required bread and milk.'

After 40 minutes, they arrived at the bakery which also appeared to be shut but, going round the back, they found the very frightened owner who recognised Jimmy James and came forward timidly.

'Why have you stopped working?' enquired Jimmy.

'Because all my men have disappeared,' replied the baker, 'and I am not able to feed the furnaces and make the bread on my own.'

'Have you got flour? Yes. OK. If I provided men, could you bake our requirements?'

'Oh yes, with help I can make the bread, but who is going to pay me?'

'Don't worry about that,' answered Bob. 'You have a contract with the camp and if you make your deliveries every other day as

115

previously, you will be paid in full. What about fuel, do you have sufficient for your furnaces?'

'Luckily, I received a delivery last week, so I am all right this month.'

'Well, I hope that we will have gone by then, so start up now. We will leave you a couple of helpers and some men to safeguard your supplies. We shall expect bread tomorrow morning. OK?'

'OK this I will do.'

Turning to Lt James, Bob asked, 'Now Jimmy, where do we go next?'

'We must head for the vegetable market which is about a mile from here.'

'If you are looking for vegetables,' interrupted the baker, 'you will find the market closed. Your best bet is to see the Mayor whose farm is the main supplier for this area.'

'And where do we find him?' asked Bob.

'You should try the Town Offices which are at the end of this street.'

So off went the group and eventually located a large red brick building which appeared to be deserted. However, in a small room at the very back, they found a manual telephone exchange which was still being operated by two elderly ladies sitting in front of a battery of cords and plugs. When Bob entered, they jumped up and cringed in the corner until it dawned on them that they were not Russians.

'Good day,' said Bob kindly. 'Please don't be afraid. We are from the prisoner-of-war camp and need your help. Can you please tell us where to find the mayor?'

Their reaction was quite startling for they both dissolved into tears and started to weep copiously. Eventually, the younger one composed herself sufficiently to answer.

'I am sorry . . . but the mayor is dead. He committed suicide last night. Can I help you?'

'Oh dear,' commented Bob, 'you see, we are here to buy fresh vegetables for our camp and were told that we should speak to the mayor.'

'That's right for the market, but it is closed. Actually, his brother manages the farm and if you will wait a minute I will see if I can connect you.'

She plugged in a cord and frantically turned a handle. When the farmer came on the line, she explained who she was and extended her sympathy on the death of his brother. She then introduced Bob and handed the extension over to him.

'Good morning sir,' he said. 'Let me introduce myself. I am Lt Conchi, a British pilot from the prisoner-of-war camp in Barth. Yesterday, the Commandant and guards of our camp marched out leaving us to fend for ourselves and I was given the job of buying vegetables from the market.'

'Well it has been closed,' commented the farmer briefly.

'Yes, I am very aware of that,' continued Bob. 'The ladies at the telephone exchange told me that you were the biggest supplier of vegetables and kindly put me through to you. Would you be prepared to supply us direct?'

'I don't see why not, but Lieutenant, would you please give me a day or two and I will come back to you. Unfortunately, my brother who was mayor, just couldn't face up to defeat by the Russians and took his life last night, and I must get into town to organise the funeral.'

'Yes, I was very sorry to hear that. Please extend our sympathy to his wife during this difficult period. Of course you must attend to family matters now. Could I contact you by telephone tomorrow?'

'Thank you, I would be most grateful. With the closing of the market, I am having to store my vegetables and would welcome an outlet before the bloody Russians arrive and commandeer them. But, how do I get paid?'

'That's no problem,' answered Bob. 'We have sufficient money to buy our immediate needs. Look, I will get our food purchaser, Lt James, to telephone you.'

It transpired that Jimmy James was able to organise the supply of fresh vegetables on the following day, so all worked out well.

During the subsequent conversation with the telephone operators, the elder of the two proudly boasted that despite everything, they had maintained a full telephone service and would continue to do so. 'Would you like to speak to your camp?' she asked. Bob was therefore able to report to Col McNeill who suggested that he should congratulate the operators and promise to provide them with a letter to the Allied Commander, praising them for services rendered. This simple action stood us in good stead next day, when we attacked the aerodrome.

Capture of Airfield

Whilst the supplies operation was in progress, a four-man reconnaissance patrol, under the command of Lt John Ramsay, was dispatched to find the most suitable route to the *Luftwaffe* airfield which lay 5 miles to the south.

'As we will be advancing in the dark, I want you to pick out landmarks that we will recognise,' commented Col McNeill. ' Be careful and don't be seen by the guards.'

The two remaining platoons, under command of further Glider Pilot officers, were now fully equipped with weapons found in the armoury. During the afternoon, they were able to fire off a few rounds to become acquainted with them.

When the reconnaissance patrol returned later that afternoon, John Ramsay was full of optimism:

> 'Sir, I had a very successful trip. The aerodrome appears to have been abandoned operationally. There are no aircraft to be seen and the gun pits round the circumference are unoccupied. Indeed, the few men observed near the main buildings were busy dismantling equipment, whilst others were towing broken-down trucks and bomb carriers onto the two runways, presumably to prevent their use. The wire round the perimeter is lightweight and is not patrolled. From my rough sketches, you will see that the control tower, offices and barrack rooms are only 300 yards inside the perimeter. We did not locate the Guard Room nor the Main Gate as these were further round to the eastern side, but I have the impression that Barth, being only a satellite field, is not protected in strength.
>
> 'The best line of approach is directly south from the camp along the road which crosses the railway line. Straight on, and after a half mile you will reach the corner of the perimeter wire. If this is followed to the east, it will lead us close to the main buildings where sleeping quarters are located. That's it sir!'"

'Good work, John,' said McNeill. Then turning to me, he said, 'Please call up my O Group.' This consisted of Lt James Mason (No 2 Platoon), Lt Ronnie Hall (No 3 Platoon), Lt Bob Conchi (No 1 Platoon), who had just returned from the supplies task and was not going to miss the assault, Lt Ramsay and myself.

'OK chaps,' said the Colonel. 'Our main objective is to capture and hold Barth aerodrome. I will now call on Lt Ramsay to repeat his report on the patrol that he has just completed.'

After receiving this, he continued.

> 'Our approach plan will be as follows: at 0400 hrs tomorrow morning, the Field Force will advance southwards towards Barth aerodrome led by the Recce Patrol followed, in open order, by No 2, No 3, Head-quarters and No 1 Platoons. Upon reaching the perimeter wire, No 2 will cut a 10-foot gap in the wire and will advance along the inside, followed by the remainder of the Force until it reaches a point from which the outline of the Administrative buildings can be seen. It will then halt and await final briefing.'

For me, I was thrilled that, after months of inactivity, I was operational once more. The following day, I was out early to form up with the assault teams. The night was clear and calm and, right on the dot of 4 o'clock, the Recce Patrol set off. They had no difficulty in following the road and soon recognised the various landmarks to reach the railway line safely. Then we passed through a nursery garden, and after 400 yards came upon the aerodrome perimeter wire on our left. James Mason had organised two sets of wire cutters and within a few minutes there was a large gap through which we passed unhindered.

The leading platoon then followed the inside of the wire which, after 450 yards, started to bend to the right. At that point Mason could just pick out the silhouette of the Control Tower, so after quietly siting the Sections, he made his way back to Headquarters where the O Group had assembled and reported to the Colonel.

> 'Sir, I have reached the position where the perimeter wire turns at right angles to the south and can just see the outline of the Control Tower and, presumably, the Administration building. I guess that they are 100 yards away. I can't see the entrance gate nor the Guard Room but assume that they are to the left of the Administration block. The whole place is quiet.'

Col McNeill thanked Mason, then gave the attack plan:

> 'No 2 Platoon will assault the Guard House and the entrance gate.
> No 3 Platoon will surround the main buildings including the sleeping quarters and capture the occupants.
> Headquarters will follow No 3 and will be located at the base of the Control Tower.
> No 1 Platoon will remain here in reserve.
> All prisoners will be put into one of the sleeping huts.
> The attack starts 0500 hrs. Report to HQ directly objectives are achieved.'

James Mason moved back to his platoon and called up the Section leaders. He explained the general plan, the platoon's task and issued orders to each Section. Looking at his watch, Mason indicated that they could start moving but to hold the actual assault until 0500 hrs. He then joined the leading Section which advanced, passing some huts 30 yards to their right. As they were ahead of schedule they slowed down slightly but then, right on time, approached a large hut which was obviously the Guard Room. To the left of it was the entrance gate where they found two elderly 'home guards' sheltering behind a pillar, chatting away and smoking happily. They must have wet their pants when confronted by black-faced soldiers speaking a strange language, but quickly accepted capture and readily surrendered their arms.

In the meantime, No 5 Section pushed open the Guard Room door to rudely waken the remainder of the guard who were dozing in arm chairs. Like the elderly men on the gate, they did not realise what had

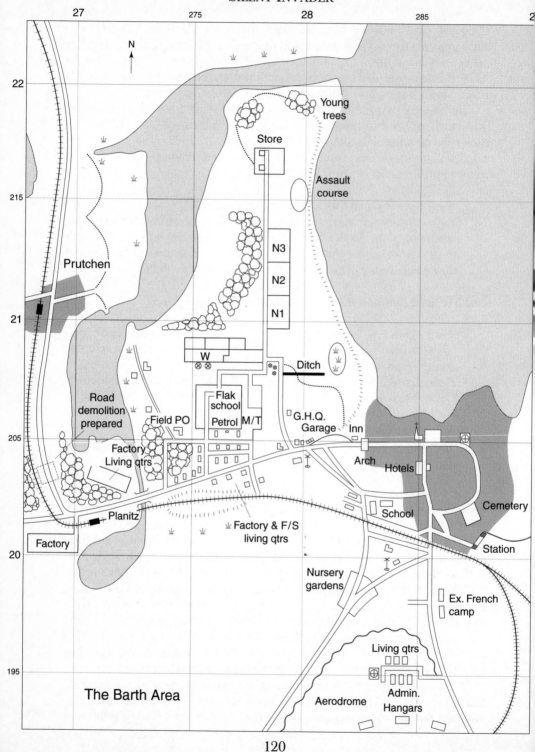

27   275   28   285

N

22

215

Young
trees

Store

Assault
course

N3

N2

N1

Prutchen

21

W

Ditch

205

Road
demolition
prepared

Field PO

Flak
school

Petrol   M/T

G.H.Q.
Garage   Inn

Factory
Living qtrs

Arch   Hotels

Cemetery

Planitz

School

Station

Factory

Factory & F/S
living qtrs

Nursery
gardens

Ex. French
camp

20

195

The Barth Area

Living qtrs

Aerodrome

Admin.

Hangars

hit them, but getting to their feet, they stood in line, hands on head, whilst they were frisked for weapons. They were a sad bunch and whilst their NCO had probably seen service in World War I, the rest hardly knew one end of a rifle from the other. At this point the two sentries were pushed in and No 2 Platoon had achieved its objective.

Whilst this was going on, No 3 Platoon had surrounded the three huts where personnel were sleeping and, rushing in, turned on the lights and called for surrender. The first two buildings had ten beds on either side with tables down the centre. The men encountered there were a much younger group who were subsequently identified as fitters. They were unarmed and obediently put on their uniforms to be herded together in the central hut.

The third building was obviously for senior personnel, and consisted of a number of single rooms of which only two were occupied. There they found two officers, one of whom seemed prepared to put up a fight, until a short burst of Schmieser fire into the ceiling made him realise he was captured. Even so, he took up an arrogant attitude, demanding to know who we were and on what authority we were acting. Needless to say, he was given short shrift and finished up being escorted outside in his pyjamas. The second officer was much older and came out of his room with hands in the air repeating 'I give up. I give up.' When asked if he spoke English he replied, 'No. I give up!' He was told to get himself a blanket and to join his colleague.

By now, Col McNeill, with Bob Conchi's platoon in reserve, had set up his Headquarters in the main room of the Control Tower and called for the two German officers to be brought to him. The elder of the two stood respectfully to attention, but the other, a pockmarked-faced individual with cropped hair, was determined to be difficult because he started to look around for a chair.

I could see that Bob was prepared to hit him and so, putting a restraining hand on his shoulder suggested that he should order the offender to stand to attention in front of a senior officer. This he did in no uncertain terms because the result was a '*Heil* Hitler' salute followed by a rigid stance. 'Now he is for it,' I thought. Bob, who has a short temper, blew his top and with a shouted 'Bastard', raised his Schmieser to club him.

'Hold it Bob,' ordered Mac. 'I want to question these two. We can sort out the insults later. Now Bob, ask who is in charge here.'

'I am,' replied the elder officer.

'Is this aerodrome operational?'

'No, it is a satellite airfield and all the aircraft have been flown out.'

'Well then, what are you doing?'

'I am an armaments officer and have 12 men with orders to make this airfield unusable for the Russians. We are busy dumping bombs on the runway which we will detonate electronically when ready.'

'You say that you have 12 men,' continued Mac, 'are they fitters? Who else is here?'

'Yes, they were responsible for rearming the guns and loading bombs into the aircraft. We had a squadron of fighter-bombers based here who flew off last week, leaving us with this dismantling job. We also have a bunch of elderly Home Guard who were supposed to ensure our safety. It looks like it, doesn't it and apart from cooks and drivers, that's the lot.'

'Well then,' said McNeill, 'you must all consider yourselves our prisoners.

'Now, I must inform you that you have been captured by a Field Force from the large *Luftwaffe* prisoner-of-war camp north of here and our objective is to hold this aerodrome and to make it serviceable so that American transport aircraft can fly in and evacuate us all later this week. You have been dismantling it which, of course, will stop immediately.

'As far as your future is concerned, I will give you two options: You can either be locked away now and handed over to the Russians when they arrive, or you can co-operate and help us to clear the runways, after which you will be released and free to get away. Which do you prefer?'

The two Germans then discussed the issue. Whilst the senior favoured co-operation and subsequent release, the younger man appeared to be completely against it and started to argue, shouting and waving his arms about.

'What is he saying Bob?' asked Mac.

'Well this bastard here says he is not going to be pushed around by a bunch of escaped prisoners. He believes that, directly the Barth police hear the aerodrome has been attacked, they will send a force to sort out "these toy soldiers", including the stuck-up Colonel. As far as he is concerned, we can get stuffed and he, for one, is not prepared to co-operate nor to stand around answering stupid questions any longer.'

Bob had hardly explained when, as if to finalise the issue, the young officer gave a Nazi salute and shouting '*Heil* Hitler', turned for the door.

'Halt!' shouted Bob. 'Stay where you are or I will shoot!'

'Don't be stupid,' came the brazen reply. 'I am a German officer and am entitled to be treated as such. I am going to get dressed.' He continued to make his exit.

'OK then, I warned you,' snarled Bob and brought up his Schmieser to fire a burst that shattered the door just as the German was reaching for the handle. For a brief moment, the shock of his near death completely paralysed the arrogant officer who then collapsed to the floor shaking visibly and, with his hands on top of his head, pleaded 'Don't shoot, don't shoot.'

'That's more like it,' responded Bob. 'Are you quite sure that you do not want to escape? Well then, turn round and crawl. Yes, crawl back here.' As the wretched man reached within a few feet he was told to halt, stand up and pay attention to the Colonel.

'Now get this into your thick head, Kraut,' commanded Mac. 'I and my Army officers here are members of the crack Airborne Division and we take no insults from arrogant Nazi thugs like you. Consider yourself lucky to be alive, but whether you will survive after we have handed you over to the Russians remains to be seen. However, as you have clearly stated that you will not co-operate, then that is your fate.'

Turning to the elder officer who looked as white as a sheet, he asked, 'What is this bastard's name and where can we lock him up?'

'He is *Lnt* Kurt Muller, my deputy. There is a cell in the Guard Room.'

'OK that is where he goes,' Mac decided. 'John, please arrange for him to be marched there and locked up. Also please check on No 2 and 3 Platoons.'

Collecting a couple of men from the reserve platoon, we frog-marched a very subdued Muller to the Guard Room where he was placed in one of the cells. There was certainly no complaints regarding officer treatment, for I think our friend had suddenly realised what he had let himself in for. As he was still only in his pyjamas, I took three blankets from the guards and thrust them at him before instructing one of the chaps to find his room and to fit him out with necessary clothes. I then had a look at the two platoons and found everything in order.

So far, five civilians had arrived for work and they were duly put in with the fitters. Whilst I was away, the senior German Officer confirmed his personal decision to co-operate and asked if he could speak to his men. This he was allowed to do after he had dressed and Bob confirmed that he had acted very properly and, in fact, had persuaded the fitters to work with us against the promise that they would be released upon completion of the task. However, Mac wanted to make the arrangement quite clear and through Bob Conchi he addressed them.

'You understand that you are now prisoners-of-war. My contract with you is that, for your freedom, you will first assist us to clear the aerodrome. You will obey my orders fully and you will not attempt to escape. Is that clear?'

Turning to the senior officer, Mac said:

'You are all on parole so let's finish the job as soon as we can. I will attach Lt Conchi to you with priority to clear the bombs. How many have you dumped so far and are they dangerous to handle? Do you require any of my men to help?'

'We have dumped about twenty on each of the two runways,' replied the officer. 'They are fused and will have to be handled carefully. It had been our plan to detonate them in pairs using the bulldozer scoop as a shield. We have a couple of bomb trailers with hand hoists that can each carry two large bombs, but it is slow work. May I suggest that you leave us responsible for handling them as my men are used to it. Your men could drive the bulldozer to push all the junk 20 metres off the runways and also to drag broken-down vehicles onto the grass.'

'That sounds OK,' commented Mac. 'Will you allocate one of your men to show us where to find equipment? I must return to the camp now but will leave Lt Mason in charge. Before I go, a few more questions. Do you know if the station radio is working?'

'Sorry I can't tell you about the radio which is in the Control Tower.'

'Is there food here for my men?'

'Yes, and I am sure that the cooks will cope with the extra numbers.'

'Finally, where is the telephone?'

'If you will please come with me, I will show you the external line.'

Mac was then put through to the telephone exchange who were pleased to connect him with Col Goodyear to whom he reported our complete success.

'Well done Mac, that's wonderful news,' came the happy response. 'Will you please stay at the aerodrome for a while. I am coming over right away with a wireless boffin to see if we can contact England. See you.'

This instruction gave Mac the opportunity of calling in the Platoon officers to issue their specific tasks. Obviously our manpower had to be concentrated upon clearing the runways and, with the German fitters working on parole, only a few men were to be used on security. It was not long before all available personnel were actively employed. I found that my job as Adjutant also embraced planning for the well-being of the Field Force and the next hour or so was spent in sorting out food for them, accommodation and blankets. I missed therefore Col Goodyear's arrival which was heralded with a blast on the motor hooter. He was 'on top of the world' and the happy outcome of the radio inspection was that, with modifications, it would be possible to contact England. Indeed, later that day, the first message was transmitted and thereafter, communication established every six hours.

After looking around briefly, Goodyear suggested that Mac and I should return with him so that we could plan our last task, namely contact with a Russian military Headquarters. This was to prove one of the most memorable experiences of my life.

THIRTEEN

CONTACTING THE RUSSIANS

Mobile Patrol

Our first foray from the camp was completed by an American Major, accompanied by one German-speaking officer and one who could speak Russian. They left in the 'jeep' festooned with a large American flag on one fender and a white flag on the other, with specific orders to examine the situation in Barth, prior to taking the main Stralsund–Rostrek road, and to wait for any signs of the Russian spearhead. They returned at midday to report.

'Barth itself,' said the Major, 'has given in and every other building is hung either with red flags or an occasional white sheet drooping from the upper floor windows.' He continued, 'We saw people standing around in pathetic groups or in doorways, wringing their hands in worry. They have obviously accepted complete and absolute defeat and are surrendering their town and themselves to the mercy of the victors. Apart from streams of refugees, there are no signs of the Russian advance, nor is there sound of gunfire to indicate any resistance.'

Later that day, a second 'mobile unit' took our vehicle and raced to the crossroads five miles south of the town to find 'Uncle Joe'. After a series of sorties around the area, they finally came upon a Russian patrol who automatically assumed that they had made contact with the Allied Army and, amidst great rejoicing, hugged and clasped hands all round. Shortly afterwards, a chunky officer, 1st Lt Karmyzoff, appeared and officially welcomed them on behalf of the Russian Republic. However, upon being informed that his contact was with aircrew from *Stalag Luft* 1, he promptly offered to travel with them to the camp to liberate it officially.

As the jeep approached the gate with horn hooting and lights flashing, the Block Commanding Officers hurried out to meet the Russian and, after much hand-shaking, retired to the Senior Officers' Mess. There, our carefully scrounged supplies of schnapps were broached to celebrate the great occasion and, through our Russian-speaking interpreter, 1st Lt Alec Nick Karmyzoff toasted the Allied victory and the destruction of Germany. Having drained his glass with one gulp, he flung it at the photograph of Hitler which hung at the end of the room, which had already been 'modified' with a huge nose and enormous donkey ears. In reply, Col Goodyear toasted 'Our solid and enduring friendship' and after drinking, followed his example.

The evening progressed with goodwill and jollity which, from the clamour within the Barrack Blocks, was equally shared by the 'kriegies' consuming their own brews distilled from raisins and prunes. Finally, with the promise to return later, our 'liberator' marched off to a nearby area which housed Russian and Polish PoWs in order to greet his countrymen. There he told them that his Regiment had fought all the way from Stalingrad and, for three years, had been in continuous battle with the Hun across Russia, Poland and now Germany. He extolled the virtues of the victorious Red Army and the new and powerful homeland which had been reborn. Finally, after more drinking, he returned to us and slept on the floor in preference to a bed that once housed a bastard Kraut!

The following morning, a very hungover Russian was driven back to his unit ostensibly to report our presence. However, as we realised that our friend was a bit of a showman and could easily be diverted from this task, it was decided that we should send a further patrol, this time to contact the Russian Army at a higher level.

Because this was to be more of a military operation, Col McNeill was instructed to arrange the necessary contact. Obviously, his personal priority was to hold and clear the aerodrome and so, after some thought, he put his hand on my shoulder and said:

> 'John, this must be your baby. First thing tomorrow, take the jeep accompanied by a German and a Russian-speaking officer and locate Brigade Headquarters. There you will report to the most senior officer that you can find and acquaint him with the situation not only in Barth, but especially at our camp and the action that we have taken to provide for our evacuation by air. I am sorry to give you this one, but quite honestly, I consider this should be an Army contact and I have got my work cut out here. I suggest that you organise your team tonight and make up a Union Jack flag to match the Stars and Stripes on the fender.'

'Thanks for your confidence in me,' I replied, grinning. 'I only hope that I can manage it without getting shot. Well, I suppose that I had better get spruced up a bit and learn a couple of phrases just to show goodwill.'

Feeling somewhat apprehensive, I went off to find Hank who spoke Russian. His parents had found their way to the States in 1919 and he had been taught by them using Russian as a home language. The second member of our team was Ted, a Flight Lieutenant from New Zealand, who had been a prisoner for nearly 4 years and who had devoted his spare time to learning and speaking German which he hoped would stand him in good stead when he finally escaped. As he was also to act as the driver, I asked him to get the jeep filled up with petrol and properly marked with the Allied stars. That evening, I found a large scale map of the area and I also raided Red Cross parcels to stock up with a plentiful supply of cigarettes. Thus equipped, we set forth early in the morning to take the road eastwards towards Stralsund.

I must confess that we started our journey with extreme trepidation and, driving slowly, approached each corner and hilltop carefully to check if Russian troops were in the vicinity. I suppose that we had travelled about 20 miles when we rounded a bend and found ourselves confronted by a company of infantry who were advancing on either side of the road.

'Stop Ted,' I called to the driver. 'Boy, this is it! Hank, it's over to you, so let's greet our friends.'

We both stood up in the jeep and, whilst shouting out words of welcome, frantically waved our flags. The immediate response from the leading soldiers was to jump into the roadside ditch to cover us with their rifles. There they remained, whilst we continued with our antics, Hank calling out in Russian and symbolically shaking his hands above his head.

'They don't seem very friendly,' commented Ted, 'shall I drive on slowly?'

'I don't think so,' I replied. 'They might misunderstand our intentions. Let them come up to us.'

Accordingly, for a long five minutes we stayed put and so did the suspicious soldiers, until finally, an NCO moved up to the leading men to find out the reason for the delay. In the meantime, Hank and I had got down from the jeep and, still waving flags, walked slowly towards the Russians calling out that we were American and British. When we reached within 50 yards from them, the message suddenly seemed to get through because the NCO jumped up and started to run towards us with his arms outstretched. Grabbing our flags, he joyfully shouted to his men that we were Allies and that, at long last, the two armies had met. As if by magic, the whole attitude of the Russians changed, for an excited crowd of about 50 rushed up to surround the jeep, with each one anxious to shake hands and clap us on the back. This moment for them was the end of the conflict, for here was evidence that the Germans had also been conquered in the west.

'Shall I tell them that we are aircrew from the nearby prisoner-of-war camp?' gasped Hank during a brief lull in the greetings.

'Not this bunch,' I replied. 'It would only involve explanations. Just say that we have to contact Brigade Headquarters and ask where we can find them.'

Hank then tried to get his information from the NCO who was really too overcome to assist. All he could do was point backwards, suggesting that they were far, far in the rear. Looking around at the soldiers, my first impression was that they were hard, seasoned fighters. Admittedly, there was no smartness about their attire for they all wore thick, loose-fitting blouses with baggy trousers tucked into their jackboots. Most were dirty and unshaven but that was understandable following weeks of battle.

After our session of backslapping, we finally returned to the jeep and with a cheery goodbye took off slowly towards the east, passing *en route* the remainder of the battalion. Our next stop was about 5 miles further on, where we approached a group of 6 tanks parked astride a cross-road. They were 'light-heavies' and certainly looked battle-scarred – muddy with strips of torn metal twisted on the bodies. Each had a large red star on the front and sides which could just be seen through the remains of branches that had once been camouflage. Their crews were obviously taking things easily because they were standing on the road enjoying a brew-up. Once again, Hank went through the procedure of greeting them with much hand-clasping and, eventually, we pulled up beside the second tank holding out the Stars and Stripes flag.

This time the reaction was immediate, and we were confronted with a bunch of cheering tank crews who milled around shouting questions. As they were a much younger and more intelligent lot, I asked if there was an officer present and when he appeared, introduced myself. Pointing to my wings, I explained, through Hank, that we were a patrol from a large airforce prisoner-of-war camp just outside Barth and our orders were to contact a senior officer at Brigade HQ. I asked if he would please tell us where to find them.

'I am afraid I can't help you,' he answered with a grin. 'We are acting as a mobile back-up for the forward infantry and all I know is that the top brass are following the advance, safe and sound and well away from the bullets! They are constantly on the move but if you continue 30 kilometres along this road towards Stralsund, you will probably locate them in comfortable quarters somewhere. Now, you tell me, how have you travelled from the west? Have you experienced any German resistance?'

'Well,' I explained, 'we are part of an armed unit that took over the camp and commandeered this jeep. There is virtually no resistance from the Germans who have surrendered Barth and you should have no trouble. I am sure you will realise it is important that we should let your people know of our existence and what we have achieved. Therefore, with your agreement, we will be on our way.' Then as a

second thought, I added, 'I don't know how your chaps are for cigarettes, but if they would like to help themselves from this box, they are
welcome.'

The officer then conveyed this gesture to his men who surged
forward to grab packets of Camel cigarettes and would have cleaned
us out had we not suggested that they had better leave some for the
other troops we were to meet. Then with good wishes for the future,
we parted company to head on eastwards.

Encounter with the Supply Corps

Our next contact was with the Supply Columns and my opinion of the
Russian soldier changed radically for they were the most uncouth men
that I have ever seen. Pure Mongolian, they were yellow-skinned, filthy
and unshaven and wrapped in all sorts of clothing, ranging from fur
coats to business suits, looted during their travels. Their means of transport typically consisted of an open flat-deck wagon pulled along by a
scraggy horse. Two of these loathsome creatures would sit huddled at
the front, whilst the wagon itself was loaded with boxes of ammunition,
together with every conceivable item of booty ranging from curtains
to eiderdowns, from women's dresses to chairs. Sitting on top of all the
junk, would be an equally filthy and degraded-looking woman who,
from her dirty, unkempt appearance, had long since given up her self
pride to serve as a slave, to forage, cook and satisfy the bestial whims
of her brutal masters.

So it was for mile after mile. There must have been hundreds of these
carts, each loaded in a similar manner. At one stage we stopped to try
and engage them in conversation but the drivers would just stare at our
interpreter through their bloodshot, slanted eyes and shrug their
shoulders. Finally we found one who excelled himself, grunting and
waving us to the rear, from which we gathered that there would be
someone further back who would understand us. Rather than show any
friendship to the stinking wretches, we continued carefully and made
our way down the line. After about three miles, we came across a
couple of NCOs standing by a motorcycle and sidecar who appeared
to be checking the wagons as they passed. They were also Mongoloid
but at least they wore some semblance of a uniform and appeared a
little more intelligent in that they could at least converse with Hank.

Despite our friendly gestures, they obviously regarded us with
extreme suspicion, as if we were fifth columnists. Only after we had
shown them our 'pass' and offered them some cigarettes did they
accept our story that we were looking for the Headquarters. Once they
had cottoned onto our wishes, they proudly told us that they knew

exactly where it was and if we followed them, they would gladly take us there. Then turning quickly, they mounted their machine and shot off in a cloud of blue smoke, the occupant of the sidecar grinning broadly as he waved us to keep up. This turned out to be far more difficult than we had anticipated, for we suddenly moved onto a track that was full of potholes. These didn't worry our guides one slightest bit as they bounced wildly from bump to bump, shrieking with laughter. Conscious that our vehicle was very precious, we followed at a more sedate pace. We drove through farmlands for a while until we eventually approached a cluster of six single-storey cottages. They were sited on either side of a cobbled yard in which there was a hand pump, together with sundry farm implements including a derelict farm cart without wheels.

'Surely there is something wrong here Hank,' I murmured, 'this is no Headquarters!'

With anxious expectancy we sat in our jeep whilst our guides joyfully indicated that we had arrived. They then dismounted and one of them entered a larger house at the end of the courtyard which we assumed belonged to the landowner as it was in a better state of repair than the rest. For a full five minutes nothing happened and I was becoming very apprehensive. Turning to our driver, I whispered, 'Ted, I think that we have got ourselves into a trap, let's get the hell out of here.' As he leant forward to switch on the ignition, a yellow hand closed on his and the second NCO who had been standing nearby, started shouting to his friend in the house who immediately rushed out with his 'tommy gun' pointed at us.

Then in heated tones he explained, 'We have first brought you to our Battalion Headquarters, because my Commanding Officer would have killed me if I had failed to do so! There will be a slight delay because the Colonel is asleep.'

'What, at 10 o'clock in the morning?' Hank queried.

'Well,' he replied with a sheepish grin, 'sort of asleep.'

Mongol Commanding Officer

Suddenly, the object of our discussion flung open one of the upper floor windows and thrusting out his large bearded face, let forth a bull-like roar, followed by a shouted instruction that we should wait until he had dressed. Then, within a couple of minutes, a veritable Goliath of man framed the doorway, grinning from ear to ear and holding out his arms in welcome.

By this time, we had moved round to stand in front of our jeep, but even at a distance of ten yards he appeared enormous. I suppose it was his head which immediately captured our attention, for it was quite grotesque. The whole face was covered by a bushy black beard that seemed to be a continuation of a mass of black curly hair which grew to within an inch of his heavy eyebrows. In turn, these met over the bridge of a large bulbous nose which showed the scars of many a fight. It was coloured in hues ranging from scarlet at the top, to a dark pitted purple at the nostrils. His mouth was partly hidden by the beard but displayed a jumble of broken, stained teeth whenever he spoke. Undoubtedly, however, the commanding feature was his jet black eyes which glared out fiercely as if to challenge anyone to disobey his wishes.

Saluting smartly, I walked towards him with the intention of shaking hands. He chose to disregard this formality and grabbed me round the waist lifting me completely off the ground. Then he proceeded to kiss me on both cheeks. With the rank smell of his breath and the roughness of his beard, it was all I could do to stop drawing away in disgust. Somehow, I managed to smile broadly and, once he had put me down, amidst roars of laughter, I grasped his hand and shook it enthusiastically. He then greeted my companions in a similar manner, shouting loudly and clapping them on their backs, before ushering us into the front room of the farmhouse.

By then, Hank had been able to explain that we were a reconnaissance patrol, that Ted and I were English and he was an American with Russian parents.

'*Engliski*' roared our giant and promptly started shaking hands once more. Then turning to one of our NCO guides, he barked out a series of instructions which Hank quietly told us had ordered him to fetch the second-in-command together with supplies of liquor with which to celebrate this memorable occasion.

Subsequently, during a rather one-sided conversation, he told us that his name was Nicholai Dzerzhinski and that he came from Ulan Bator in Mongolia. He was in charge of a regiment of the Army Supply Corps which had followed the front line right across the continent and, as far as he was concerned, his ambition was to grind the bloody Germans into the dust so that they would never rise as a race again. To underline his views, he than spat on the floor.

Jokingly, we tried to pronounce Dzerzhinski and finally asked if we could settle for 'Uncle Nick' as he closely resembled someone of that name! This tickled his sense of the ridiculous because he collapsed in a cascade of raucous guffaws, his whole frame shaking as he repeated 'Uncle Nick'.

At this stage, his second-in-command, a tough little man with bowed legs and a voluminous backside, came into the room with a cardboard box full of bottles. After introducing him to us, the colonel insisted that

we should also give him a nickname. After some discussion, we chose
'Cousin Rump' explaining that he resembled a famous character from
the fairy tale 'Rumpelstiltskin'. The fact that his posterior matched the
name was not mentioned and the party started with a vengeance with
toasts all round.

I had no idea what we were drinking, but it was certainly a fierce
white spirit which burned the throat and I quickly realised that we
would have to take it quietly as over-indulgence would end in an early
collapse. Fortunately, 'Uncle Nick' was far too busy replenishing his
own glass to notice that we either didn't finish ours or that it was surrep-
titiously emptied into the fern. After about an hour of continuously
toasting everyone that we could think of, our noisy host lurched to his
feet to announce proudly that we were all the victors and as such, were
now entitled to relax to enjoy three basic pleasures, drink, food and
women. As the chosen officer in the Red Army to welcome the first
British and Americans, he would do his very best to ensure that these
needs were satisfied.

Clapping his hands, he called in one of his men and issued a string
of orders and then returned to the problem of finishing every bottle in
sight. Sidling over to Hank, I asked what had been said, but he
confessed that he had not been able to understand much of the order,
except that food was to be prepared. This came as welcome news as
we hadn't eaten for hours, and certainly needed some 'blotting paper'
for all the drink consumed.

Noises from the kitchen, including much shouting and the occasional
female yelp, ultimately culminated with a corporal pushing in two terrified women bearing steaming bowls of vegetable soup with platters of
rye bread and cheese. The corporal, through Hank, apologised for the
sparseness of the meal, but assured us that for supper, he would round
up some chickens for a stew. The bowls had hardly been handed out
when the great hulk of a man picked up his and, with a huge swallow,
finished the lot to ask for more. I must admit that, whilst the soup was
somewhat greasy, when it was supped with the black bread, it proved
to be quite tasty. Similarly, the local cheese added a flavour that I had
missed for months.

During the meal, Uncle Nick and his second-in-command continued
to toss down the fiery liquid as if it was water. With each glass
consumed, so their laughter and shouting became louder and coarser.
Every now and then, our host would have a fit of uncontrollable
coughing which would start as a chest rumble, becoming louder and
louder, until with a final heave, he would clear his throat and eject a
stream of thick yellow phlegm onto the floor. He would then gasp for
air, wipe his filthy mouth with the back of his hand and pick up his
glass once more. I was nearly sick each time this happened and was

quite relieved when he staggered to the front door, beckoning us to follow.

At first I thought his hospitality had come to an end and that we would be taken on to Brigade Headquarters. To his mind, however, it was only just beginning, for assembled in the yard, on either side of the derelict wagon, were two groups of frightened peasants. Six women with small children huddled together for comfort formed one group, whilst two old men and a couple of boys formed the other. Upon sighting their Commanding Officer, the Russian soldiers screamed an order and promptly followed it up by laying about the wretched groups with their rifle butts until they formed two lines. Strutting down the centre, glaring at the two lines who visibly cringed under his stare, the Colonel mounted the wagon and proceeded to harangue his captive audience in Russian. His tirade was first translated by Hank into English and then by Tim into German:

'You will now understand that the English, American and Russian soldiers have met on the Baltic and that it will only be a couple of days before the whole of Germany is conquered. The German army is beaten ... the German people are beaten and will now be treated as the servants of the victorious Allies until such time as they learn how to behave. You men will work on the farm to provide food, you boys will cut wood to keep us warm and you women will be allocated duties to serve, without question, the wishes of your Russian masters.

'To start off, I propose to show my generosity to the three officers who have honoured me this morning, by giving them first choice of the women present and woe betide any one of you who does not meet their slightest demands. Do you understand you bitches? Answer me ... do you understand?'

The wretched females whimpered and cringed, nodding their heads in acceptance. He stepped down and slowly moved down the line of shivering women, stopping in front of each to make lewd comments about their looks, their figure and their probable performance in bed. Halting by a young girl of about 22, who stood trembling with her head bowed, he grabbed her by the hair and, with a vicious pull, yanked her face upwards so that she was forced to look into his eyes. 'You ungrateful slut,' he yelled, 'you ought to be proud to serve heroes like these!' With his other hand, he ripped her dress down to her waist. Letting out a scream of terror, the pathetic girl fell onto her knees to plead for mercy, only to receive a push which left her prostrate on the ground.

This treatment proved too much for one of the farm labourers who scrambled forward to try and stop the Colonel. With hardly a pause, the giant of a man thrust a huge hand into the face of his 'would be' attacker and followed it up with a shattering chop onto the side of his neck. With a howl of agony the poor man collapsed in a heap, to be promptly set upon by two of the soldiers who clubbed his inert body with their rifles until they tired. Then they dragged the terribly bruised and unconscious creature to the side as a warning to others who might be prompted to interfere.

By this time, every single woman together with their children, had been reduced to a state of hysteria, whilst the object of the original attack lay grovelling on the cobbles frantically trying to cover her naked breasts by holding together the shreds of her pathetic dress. Watching this bestial display, I was overwhelmed with disgust and in an effort to end the girl's agony, called out, 'OK Uncle Nick. I will take this one.' With a roar of laughter, he acclaimed my choice and, pulling the girl to her feet by her hair, thrust the terrified woman into my arms. After the performance had been repeated for my two associates, the Colonel marched off towards the farmhouse and with a grandiose gesture, bowed low at the doorway as if to indicate the hospitality was ours for the asking.

Realising my hopeless position in the hands of this barbarian, I grasped the shivering girl by the arm and guided her towards the room where we had been drinking, beckoning the others to follow. Both Hank and Tim appeared to be equally embarrassed about the situation, but quickly cottoned onto my hastily prepared plan as I turned to face our host. Standing smartly to attention and with an exaggerated salute, I called on Hank to interpret my speech of appreciation.

'Colonel, we, the representatives of the British and American Armies, acclaim you as a true symbol of the mighty and triumphant Russian nation and we salute you.' My two colleagues then aligned themselves and joined the ridiculous performance. 'We hail your victories and are proud that we had the honour of meeting such a magnificent soldier who, amongst his many duties, has found the time to entertain us magnificently and to provide so fully for our comfort.'

At this stage Nick, quite overcome by the pompous address, moved forward with arms outstretched to embrace me in yet another hug, but recognising that we were still standing at the salute, halted a yard away and brought his hand up to his forehead to return the compliment. This gave me the chance to continue:

'Now Colonel, we are soldiers like yourself and we place our country before our very lives. Our country orders us to make contact with the nearest Russian General as soon as possible . . . so may I make a suggestion. Let us first report to Brigade Headquarters and then return to you to enjoy at our leisure and without having to hurry, the pleasures that you have promised us.'

Fortunately, it worked, for in his reply, still at the salute, he assured me that in the Russian Army too, duty came first. Therefore he would see that we were safely delivered to his General and the guide would stay over to return us to the most memorable evening of our lives. With that, he shouted a stream of instructions which finally culminated with the arrival of the Orderly Room Clerk with a letter of introduction which was duly signed and handed to me.

Whilst all these arrangements were in hand, the three women, still in a state of complete fear, sat huddled in a group whimpering and contemplating their fate at the hands of the conquerors. At my suggestion, Tim walked over and told them not to worry and when we left, to slip away and hide. Whether the plan worked for them, I shall never know, as I didn't have the slightest intention of returning to that nightmare.

FOURTEEN

MEDAL PARADE

Russian Brigade Headquarters

The Mongol second-in-command jumped into the front of the jeep and amidst shouts of farewell, accompanied with assurances of our return, we roared off in a cloud of dust. Our route took us back onto the main road where we turned east for about 7 miles before arriving at the gates of what appeared to be a walled estate. These were locked and guarded by a Section of tough-looking soldiers who surveyed the arrival of a strange vehicle with extreme suspicion.

Despite his rank, 'Cousin Rump' nervously descended from the jeep and, waving the letter of introduction at the Sergeant of the guard, tried to explain that we were British and American officers who wished to see the Brigadier. Accordingly, would he please unlock the gates and permit us through.

'*Niet*' came the blunt reply and no amount of persuasion would make him change his mind. He was not going to admit anyone and that was that. Poor old 'Rump' came back to us in despair and full of apologies for our treatment. As we just had to see someone, I suggested that Hank should now approach the guard waving the Stars and Stripes flag and ask if any officer could come to the gates to see us. This new tactic finally got us somewhere because the Sergeant reluctantly left us under the watchful eye of a soldier whilst he retired to the gate-house to telephone someone in authority. After a while, he came back to announce that an officer was on his way. Ten minutes later a staff car pulled up at the gates and a smartly dressed captain jumped out to approach us via the side door. In the meantime we had lined up and, as he neared us, came to a smart salute whilst I announced my rank and name.

'Greetings friends,' he said in English, 'at long last we meet in our victory.'

Realising the understandable error, I hastily explained that we were a reconnaissance patrol from a large aircrew PoW camp at Barth with orders to contact the most senior Russian officer.

'Well, you are certainly most welcome and you couldn't have come at a better time because our General is at Brigade Headquarters this afternoon to present medals "in the field". He should be finished shortly and then you can meet him.'

Turning aside, he clapped his hands to order the guards to open the gates and then suggested that I should travel with him whilst the others followed. Having settled me in the front, he introduced himself as Capt Pieter Petrov and explained he was the Brigade Intelligence Officer. He proudly declared that he could speak five languages but apologised that his English was not 'so very good'.

'It sounds pretty fluent to me,' I replied. 'One of my officers, Hank here, is an American pilot who speaks Russian, so we should get along well.'

With that settled, he let in the clutch and drove up a long drive towards a large three-storey mansion set in gardens which stood back from and overlooked a paved area about 40 yards square. On three sides, stood lines of smartly dressed officers and other ranks, whilst at the head there was a dais upon which there was a trestle table covered with a large Red Army flag. Our guide quietly pulled up on the edge of the square and from this vantage point, we watched a sturdy and very tough-looking officer, with a chest full of ribbons, present medals to the worthy recipients. As each had the decoration pinned on his chest, he would salute and be sent on his way with a friendly pat on the back from the General. It was a very smart and impressive occasion but spoilt by the fact that the loudspeaker system was making the most peculiar noises and, despite the frantic efforts of an electrician, was finally shut off altogether.

At the end of the ceremony, one of the senior officers stepped forward to lead their equivalent of 'Three cheers for the General'. Then amidst much back-slapping, the decorated men moved into the mansion to celebrate. Quickly, Captain Petrov, who had been keeping up a running commentary throughout the proceedings, leapt out of the car and ran towards the gathering of senior officers who had surrounded the General. Quite obviously the news of our presence caused a bit of a stir, because the group suddenly parted and the little man, followed by a phalanx of his staff, marched purposefully towards us.

Once again, out little contingent lined up in front of our beflagged jeep and, on my command, stepped forward to salute in unison, to which the General responded but followed it up with a series of bear hugs. Then, grabbing me by the arm and with the Intelligence Officer on the other side, he practically frog-marched me up the steps into the large hall of the house.

This was a room about 80 feet long with little alcoves leading off to the various living areas. It was dominated by a wide staircase at the far end which was flanked by a heavy balustrade, whilst around the walls there were a number of tapestries along with large paintings of previous members of the family, who gazed on the motley gathering.

With much gesticulation and friendly banter, my new host insisted upon introducing me to every member of his entourage, during which stage it was noticed that I was wearing Glider Pilot wings and had an Airborne flash on my uniform. When I explained that I was a Glider Pilot in the British Airborne forces, the General immediately instructed Petrov to find food and drink and to join us on a couch in one of the alcoves.

Pointing once more to my wings, he exclaimed, 'A Glider Pilot eh? We don't have gliders, so you must tell me all about them and how they are used in battle.'

'Well sir,' I replied, speaking slowly so that Petrov could interpret, 'I command a Flight of gliders and on D-Day, we flew in a Company of infantry of the 6th Airborne Division who were part of a force whose task was to provide immediate protection for the eastern flank of the beachhead and to counter any German attack.'

'Were you involved in heavy fighting?' he interrupted.

'On that invasion no, because the Glider Pilots were pulled out after a couple of days to pick up fresh aircraft and to fly in the 1st Airborne Division. The original plan was to leapfrog the Airborne Divisions but, as you may remember, the Germans held up the advance at Caen. So the 1st Division was next used at Arnhem and on that battle, we carried an Anti-tank Battery with their jeeps, trailers and 6-pounder guns.'

'Ah yes,' commented my host, 'somewhere I read that gliders also transported small tanks into battle. Did you?'

'No sir, that was the Hamilcar, a much larger glider than the Horsa which was generally used. They were designed to carry a tank but were later employed for heavy vehicles. We didn't see many of them at Arnhem.'

'Talking of Arnhem,' continued the General, 'please tell all about your own part in the battle.' So it was that, for the next 20 minutes, I related my story and the help given by the Dutch.

'What an experience,' was the comment. 'I can assure you that, even at my level, there have been times when I was stranded, but luck in the form of the German mistakes or even the weather, has enabled me to extricate my forces. Anyway, to get back to your battle, what went wrong? I mean to say, despite all sorts of claims that much had been achieved, the whole operation was really a failure wasn't it?'

'Unfortunately, sir, I am not able to answer on the "whole operation" as I do not have all the facts available. I assume that the British XXX Corps made the planned crossings at Eindhoven and Nijmegen satisfactorily but ran into trouble after that. As far as Arnhem is concerned, having been on the receiving end of the German counter-attack, I can only give you a personal opinion that something definitely went wrong! The 1st Airborne Division was expected to seize and hold the main bridge over the Rhine for 48 hours, which time would have been sufficient for the Guards Armoured Division to sweep through and to turn the Siegfried Line from the north-west. This we did against all odds, but after nine days, Montgomery was still 17 km away and not able to relieve us. I used the phrase "against all odds" because the major factor which turned the tables in our fight to hold the bridge, was the presence of large numbers of heavy Tiger tanks which had not been anticipated and against which we had little or no defence.

'Speaking to other Glider Pilots who had been in the thick of things, they confessed that it had been a terrifying experience as these huge tanks, using their guns and flamethrowers, simply demolished the buildings that they occupied. The Anti-tank Battery that my Flight had carried had some success but were soon outnumbered and liquidated, leaving the wretched infantry with the task of coping with the German troops that followed behind.

'Ammunition and food was short and sadly, resupply fell into the hand of the Germans but somehow we held on, although the worst personal aspect was waiting for the relieving army who never came!'

At this stage, the Chief of Staff approached cautiously, pointing to his watch to indicate that it was time to move on. However, the General waved him away and continued to seek my views on a number of subjects whilst, to my concern, Petrov brought further supplies of drinks. It was during one of his many deliveries that he caught his foot on the rug and overbalanced, losing control of the tray. As I could see the drinks were going to finish up on the General's lap, I leapt up to grab a couple of the falling bottles but, in doing so, poured beer onto the crutch of his uniform. Quite overcome by the mess that I had made, I was full of apologies, which were met with a roar of laughter from the General. 'Tell this young man that it won't be the first time that I have wet my pants.'

After stewards had mopped up, the General then asked me about our camp, but as I was about to reply, he held up his hand and called over Colonel Zchervynick who was to take over as Commander of the district of Barth.

'Ah Comrade Colonel,' said the General. 'The captain here was about to tell me about their large camp containing British and American aircrew and as you will obviously be involved with them, I thought that you should also hear what he has to say.'

'Well sir,' I recounted, 'over the last few months, we created a Field Force and we trained and equipped 50 men with Glider Pilots as officers. When the Germans announced that we were to march to the south, we overwhelmed them. With the resulting weapons and those captured from the Flak School nearby, we took over the bakery and vegetable supplies and then captured the *Luftwaffe* aerodrome. The German squadrons had abandoned the place but had left behind sappers to blow up sections of the two runways. Fortunately we were in time to stop them and radioed England to arrange our evacuation by air, even though the war was still in progress.'

The General was tickled pink that prisoners-of-war had actually taken the offensive against the Hun and insisted that an immediate liaison be established with his forces. Turning to Col Z he said, 'We must help these fellows. After the party, I want you to return with this young man and meet the senior American and British officers.'

In passing, he asked if we had any food problems and I explained that whilst we were all right for the moment, we really needed fresh meat and vegetables. Again turning to Col Z, he instructed him to take immediate action and sure enough, within 36 hours, a hundred head of cattle were herded into our camp compound.

By this time the party was becoming somewhat noisy and I caught sight of Hank and Ted, frantically trying to support each other in their interpretation of a Cossack dance, much to the hilarious enjoyment of their new friends. When the General was finally induced to make his departure, I suggested to Col Z that as he had quite a trip to Barth and back, it might be wise for us to leave also. He agreed and offered to explain to 'Rump' of the Supply Corps that we were still on duty and would not be able to return with him. Having collected my erstwhile Cossacks, we made our farewells and steered an unsteady but very correct course back to our vehicle where the Colonel had already assembled a couple of cars to carry members of his staff including Pieter, our English-speaking friend.

Russian Help

Fortunately, once back on the main road, our journey was comparatively easy and we reached the camp just as it was approaching dusk. Leaving the Russians in the care of Hank, I made my way to the senior officers' quarters where I found Col Goodyear and hurriedly acquainted him with the situation, whilst he hastily changed into his uniform.

'Well done, young Morrison,' said the chief. 'As you started this, you had better be in on the talks, especially as Mac has had to go out to the aerodrome.' Thus it was than an exhausted Glider Pilot spent the next two hours fighting off sleep, whilst his seniors discussed the problems of the joint control of the area.

Right from the start, Col Z and his staff were most co-operative.

Amongst other issues, it was arranged for every member of the Field Force to carry a pass, written in Russian, authorising him to be in the Barth area between 10 a.m. and 9 p.m. The Platoon Commanders and liaison officers like myself received a card signed by Col Z, instructing Russian soldiers to render any assistance necessary.

During a lull in the discussions, our chief turned to me and quietly asked if I could think of any gesture that he could make in return for the help offered by the Russians. I suggested that, apart from a personal gift of a carton of cigarettes each, they might welcome some help with their public address system at Brigade Headquarters. I went on to tell of the débâcle during the medal parade and pointed out that the equipment at the Flak School was now redundant.

Latching onto the idea, Col Goodyear commented, 'Morrison here was telling me about the fine medal ceremony that he witnessed but which had been spoilt by the failure of the loudspeakers.'

'Yes, that was a shame,' replied Col Z, 'but I fear that years of being on the move, hasn't improved the equipment.'

'I only mention it because we have recently stripped the system out of the Flak School next-door and would be very happy to send over a couple of technicians to show your people how to operate it.'

Col Z was delighted and looking round at me, expressed the hope that I would also re-visit Brigade Headquarters next day to meet some of his officers. Feeling a bit embarrassed that I was being singled out, whilst my own boss in the Field Force was away, I respectfully suggested that perhaps that he should make contact and this was promptly accepted. Accordingly, on the following day, Hank drove Col McNeill over to Brigade HQ with the two radio men, a ploy that was to prove invaluable a few days later.

Before leaving, Col Z arranged that he and his staff would visit the camp for a brief meeting every other day at 10 o'clock, to sort out any problems that we might have. On that happy note they pushed off.

Trouble at the Aerodrome

Unfortunately, as often happens when things appear to be going well, a situation developed at the aerodrome which was to delay the clearing of the runways. It seems that, on the previous evening, *Lnt* Schmidt, the senior German officer, had approached Lt John Mason, the Glider Pilot in charge.

'Lieutenant, may I ask you a great favour?' he said. 'If I stand personally responsible for *Lnt* Kurt Muller, would you consider releasing him on parole? I should explain that he is absolutely repentant for his behaviour two days ago and is terrified at the prospect of being handed over to the Russians, as this will probably result in his being shot. He has appealed to me to ask forgiveness and promises to strive to the utmost to justify your pardon.'

'He's got a bloody nerve to beg forgiveness,' interrupted Bob, 'as far as I am concerned, the Nazi swine deserves to be shot!'

'I can understand your feelings,' Schmidt replied, 'but I am battling to finish the job as soon as possible and I could certainly use him to supervise one of the bomb removal squads.'

'I shall have to ask Col McNeill,' said Mason, 'and will let you know.'

'I think that you are making a mistake,' persisted Bob. 'I don't trust the bastard, but, if we do release him on parole, let's have an armed guard with his bomb team.'

Having broached the issue with Mac, it was decided that, with the senior officer's assurance of good behaviour, we might benefit from this gesture. So it was that Muller was released from the Guard Room and, with great humility asked to apologise to Bob personally. Although it was accepted, Bob suggested that Flt Lt Mike Horne should accompany the team as he could speak a little German and could check on the 'reformed' character. Throughout the day, Muller worked well and enthusiastically and possibly this fact lulled Horne into being over-confident.

Towards evening, the team were using six-foot wooden poles to lever a fairly heavy bomb onto the trolly. As they did so, it began to move and Muller asked Horne to apply the brake. However, when he bent down to do this, Muller brought up his pole and struck Horne a heavy blow on the head which half-stunned him and he dropped his rifle. Muller promptly picked it up and, holding it at the prostrate man's head, told him to be quiet. The incident had obviously been preplanned because the gang dragged the injured man to the bomb trolly and, having tied his hands and stuffed a rag into his mouth, they roped him securely to the wheels. Then, with smug '*Heil* Hitlers', they all scuttled off to the perimeter wire and disappeared. The first that Mason heard of the escape was when a very contrite and worried German Officer reported at dusk that Muller's team had not returned.

'I told you that the bastard could not be trusted,' fumed Bob.

'Yes you did,' admitted Mason. 'I suppose they have buggered off. I wonder what has happened to Mike?'

Then turning to *Lnt* Schmidt he said, 'It seems that your men cannot be trusted when they are on parole so, from now on, they will be treated as prisoners. They will be locked in their rooms when not working and will be shot if attempting to escape. Because your numbers are reduced and I now have to use some of my chaps as guards, we will all start work earlier and work until dusk. I want you to explain the position to your men right now and let them know that the tough treatment has been brought about by the dishonesty of their associates. Bob, will you please go along and make sure that this message gets over properly.'

John Mason then arranged the posting of the necessary guards for the evening meal. Then he called on the tractor-driver to take a couple of armed men with him and drive down the runway on which Muller's team had been working. After 500 yards, the search party came upon the bomb trolly and upon closer inspection found the huddled figure of Mike Horne lashed to it. Upon releasing him from his bonds, they were subjected to a tirade of swearing about the German race, and the parentage of *Lnt* Muller in particular.

'The bastard Nazi jumped me when I was helping and knocked me out,' he moaned. 'If I ever catch him, he won't last a minute! I am terribly sorry John.'

'Never mind Mike, you were conned. Let me have a look at your head. Goodness me, you have a lump as big as an egg where he hit you. Go and lie down and I will see if I can find some pills to help ease the pain.'

John Mason then telephoned the camp and reported to Col McNeill who had just returned from his visit to Brigade HQ.

'Don't worry John,' commented Mac. 'I doubt if the escapees are interested in anything other than getting as far away from the Russians as possible. The town of Barth has surrendered and the police have disappeared, so things should be quiet for you. Nevertheless, you are getting a little thin on the ground and I will transfer a platoon to you tomorrow. I will now collect some pills from the Camp Doctor and bring them over. See you in an hour or so.' This immediate reaction from the Colonel was yet another example of the care and attention he gave to the men under his command.

Without doubt, work at the aerodrome was a hard slog and great credit was due to the gallant men for sticking to the backbreaking task. It is understandable that, as there were no lights in the barracks, some of the chaps when 'off standby', made their way into Barth to sample the local brew and anything else that might be available. Having no money, it was a case of simple barter. As most of the Germans had not seen real coffee and tea for many years, some successful bargains were negotiated. One of the wilder officers happily announced that, after a couple of beers, he had spent the evening in the company of a lovely blonde, and all for a tin of sardines!

FIFTEEN

CONCENTRATION CAMP

French Survivors

One afternoon, whilst driving to the aerodrome to check on the progress, I came across a group of what appeared to be three hospital inmates trying to climb over the perimeter wire. Drawing up alongside, I called on them to stop, at which they dropped to the ground. Prostrating themselves, they appealed for mercy. I had Ted with me, but his efforts at German produced blank stares until one, who appeared to be the leader, raised himself up on his hands and started to address us in humble terms. Suddenly, it dawned on me that he was speaking French. I replied, telling the miserable specimens to stand up and approach us.

My assumption that they were hospital internees stemmed from the fact that they looked so haggard and hardly had an ounce of flesh on their bones. Indeed, on closer inspection, they resembled walking skeletons with wobbly heads, from which large bloodshot eyes glowed in lassitude. From their frames, if that is what one could call the emaciated bodies, hung vertical-striped uniforms, similar to heavy pyjamas, which trailed on the ground to encompass their feet. Quite obviously, they assumed they were going to be punished and it took some time to persuade them that they would not be hurt. Suspiciously they edged forward as if expecting a malicious trap, only taking the final steps when we offered them a cigarette.

Even after the bliss of their first smoke, they could not accept that we wished them no harm and our attempts of showing them the Union Jack didn't register any message. However, slowly they realised we were not Germans and they finally agreed to get into the jeep and be driven to the aerodrome. There they were given sweet tea and bread which they ate ravenously. Only then, were we able to learn their story.

In short, after the fall of France, able-bodied young men had been rounded up and press-ganged into labour camps where, in miserable conditions, they were given backbreaking tasks such as digging tunnels. Later, as the demand for labour continued, their Nazi masters delved deeper and segregated those who might be considered as leaders (e.g. lawyers, doctors and teachers) including these senior citizens and they were also sent to camps to tackle work for which they were completely unsuited. The result was that only half of them survived; apart from the long hours with little food, they were always at the mercy of French hirelings who held their status positions solely through continuous displays of bestiality. The ones that survived would be transferred from camp to camp as the jobs changed, and the three that we had found had been sent to Barth about nine months previously. It transpired that the leader was a doctor and his two friends acted as medical orderlies in a camp where, somehow, they tried to care for the sick.

As with ourselves, the Germans had left some six days previously, making no effort to provide the prisoners with food. Most of those who were able had already taken their chance of making their way back to France, or at least to the Allied lines by living off the countryside. However, there were still about 40 men in the camp, either too weak or too sick to attempt the journey, and the doctor and his assistants had stayed behind to look after them. Their main problem was food and today's foray into the *Luftwaffe* camp was to try and scrounge something. On the previous day they had walked into Barth to beg for food, but had been chased off by angry citizens who were not the slightest bit interested in the fact that men were starving within two miles of their homes.

Although these poor prisoners were not our responsibility, I felt a strong desire to help. At least we had food, and so we loaded up with as many tins of soup and stew as we could spare, before taking off for the bakery where, as luck would have it, I was able to commandeer twenty long loaves. Then, with our three inmates, who incidentally had found the opportunity to have a wash, we made for their camp.

It was the smell that first alerted us that we are approaching the camp. The fetid stench of rotting flesh, the general filth and the sewage seemed to pervade the whole area. As we drove through the gates into a deserted compound, I was conscious of huge piles of muck and rubbish everywhere. Those who had already departed had dumped filthy bedding together with overturned night buckets on what had previously been their parade ground, and we had to drive through this stinking slush to reach the Sick Quarters. There we saw some of the wretched prisoners who had virtually consigned themselves to a slow and lingering death. They lay out in the open on mattresses in front of the medical block, in the belief that, if they stayed near the doctor, they would surely be saved.

Wisely, they were told that we were Allied officers and that help was on the way. Otherwise, I am sure that we would have been mobbed by the starving crowd. We were thus able to drive round to the back of the building to unload the food without interruption. Whilst this was in progress, I took a quick look into the only ward, in which there were 16 beds occupied by feeble and motionless skeletons in various stages of death. Crammed in-between on the floor, were other mounds of human beings wrapped in filthy blankets and crying in vain for any form of relief – even a speedy dispatch. It was quite pathetic and I greatly admired the doctor and his assistants for their personal sacrifice in staying behind. Once the rations had been unloaded and some form of distribution organised, we made our departure, promising to visit them the following day with the camp medical team who would also bring medicines and drugs.

During a subsequent discussion with the doctor, I discovered that the French Concentration camp had originally housed up to 500 prisoners in appalling conditions, sleeping two to a bunk with often two in-between on the floor. Food was given only to those who worked and officially, the sick received nothing. However, in practice, friends would help out, which, in effect, meant that nearly everyone was on a starvation level. Even so, within each block, there were thugs who demanded 'protection dues' and failure to pay up promptly would often result in a 'ducking'. That is to say, at night the defaulter would be picked up bodily and plunged head down into the night bucket full of urine. No-one would dare lift a hand to help him and the semi-unconscious wretch would then be left wet and filthy until the following morning. Fortunately the doctor and his assistants had been free from harrassment and were able to scrounge extra food for themselves and patients by 'cooking the books' on fatalities.

It is pleasing to record that, with the help of our MO and subsequently the Russian Ambulance Corps, most of these men were restored to reasonable health and presumably to their families.

Female Slave Labour

The release of the second 'forced labour' camp presented quite a different and frightening experience. Lt Bill Sykes, who was my Flight's second-in-command, had been made responsible for the camp's security and, as such, commanded a Company of armed pilots who not only manned the defence system but also patrolled the vicinity of the camp. For some time, we had been aware that there was a prison factory about a mile to the west of *Stalag Luft* 1 and from the baker, who had a contract to supply bread, we learnt that there were about 70 women political prisoners there, working and living in dreadful

146

conditions. As there were no apparent problems with the security in the camp, Col McNeill ordered Bill to go with a Section of his men to investigate the true position and to take any necessary steps to release the prisoners.

Accordingly, they marched off early the next morning accompanied by a Polish pilot who spoke a little German. Bill was back by midday looking as white as a sheet to report on his distressing experience.

'Col McNeill, I have just seen the most appalling example of slave labour but worse, the vicious and terrible whiplash of revenge by those who previously suffered. It was unbelievable.'

'Take it quietly Bill and let's hear the story.'

Bill then gave his account:

> 'Well, we marched to the factory which is surrounded by an 8-foot wire fence. I suppose there were about six wooden huts sited around a large two-storey brick building. At the entrance there was a barbed-wire gate guarded by a tough looking wardress, who, when we approached, promptly proceeded to chain and lock it before disappearing into the guard hut. As our shouts to attract her fell on deaf ears, we lifted the gate off its hinges and went to sort her out. At first she refused to speak to us, but after the door was forced open and she had received a couple of whacks on her backside for her rudeness, she decided to co-operate and to take us to the "person in command". This turned out to be a hatchet-faced Amazon wearing a uniform of a prison officer.
>
> 'Who the hell are you,' she shouted.
>
> 'You keep a civil tongue when you speak to me,' I retorted. 'Firstly, are you in command?'
>
> 'Yes, I am the Chief Wardress of this Labour Camp. I have 66 women here from various countries who are all enemies of the Third Reich. In view of their criminal actions, I and my staff, operate this factory as a prison where they are expected to work hard to pay for their food and keep. I propose to . . .'
>
> 'You don't propose anything,' I interrupted,' because you are no longer in charge. Germany is beaten and you will release the prisoners immediately. Do you understand?'
>
> 'No I don't,' she shouted back, sticking out her chin in defiance. 'I only take orders from my superior officers.'
>
> 'OK,' I said. 'Lock her up in the guard room and we will hand her over to the Russians to sort her out.'
>
> 'The Russians?' Her jaw dropped and she sank back in her chair like a pricked balloon. 'Why the Russians?'
>
> 'Because they will soon be your "superiors" and will know how to deal with an arrogant bitch like you.'

147

'Please,' she pleaded, 'I am innocent. I only obey orders. What do you want?'

'I want to see what these people are doing and I want them freed,' I replied.

'All right, please come with me.' Picking up a bunch of keys, she walked towards the brick building.

At the first door, she stopped and turned the key in the lock and stood on one side, ushering my Section into a long hall-like room with a conveyor line down the centre. Seated on either side of the rubber belt were about 20 women, each with a deep tray containing a mixture of coal dust and wet clay beside them. Mechanically, they would reach into it and scoop up a handful to mould it into a cake, which was then carefully placed on the conveyor to take it into the drying room. The whole area was enveloped in a cloud of coal dust which had settled on the faces and hair of the sweating workers so that they looked filthy and degraded. For a few moments the Section stood dumbstruck watching the pitiful scene as the sallow, hollow-cheeked and completely apathetic creatures slumped over their menial task, whilst the vicious supervisors strutted up and down, swearing and lashing out with their leather straps. I then ordered that the conveyor should be stopped and as the Chief Wardress switched it off, the prisoners looked up for the first time as if to expect further abuse.

Then, moving up to the end of the line, I rapped on the table to get their attention and called out that we were British and American soldiers who had come to set them free. As there was no response, Hans, my interpreter, repeated the message in German and French. I suppose that I had to repeat the news three times before it finally sank in and then, with shrill shouts, they jumped up from their benches with tears of happiness streaming down their faces. Soon they were dancing around with complete abandon, absolutely delirious with joy. Finally, in exhaustion, they sat down again, laughing and giggling between themselves.

Suddenly, as if a common thought had transmitted itself, they turned to see their guards creeping out of the door. With one accord they rushed after them like devils possessed, screaming "kill them . . . kill them." Realising their danger, the wardresses took to their heels but there were too many "hunters" and those who were caught were flung to the ground and set upon viciously with anything that came to hand, such as boards, bricks, clogs. They used anything to destroy their tormentors' lives. In vain the wardresses pleaded for mercy but, by now, the lust for killing had taken over and there were groups of five or six women frantically trying to maim and obliterate each semi-conscious body that was held down. Some of the mob smashed their faces to a pulp using bricks to break noses and teeth, whilst others ruthlessly gouged out their eyes. Not satisfied, they then held the noses of each guard and forced the coal dust mixture down their throats until they could no longer breathe and passed out.

I know the bitches all deserved to be punished but to stand there and witness the ghastly retribution was too much for me and so I fired warning shots into the air and shouted at them to stop. I might as well have saved my ammunition for each and every prisoner was determined to take her personal revenge and despite our efforts to pull them off, they would immediately be replaced by others. Eventually, one of the lads found some fire extinguishers with which we sprayed the groups thus temporarily halting the slaughter when they fell back coughing and spluttering. This enabled us to recover the horribly mutilated bodies on the promise that the one who still appeared to be alive would be handed over to the Russians. What happened to the Chief Wardress, I shall never know, because she must have made a quick getaway, but I hope her soul rots in Hell.

Finally, when things had settled down a little, I explained that we could only offer them temporary food and leave it to them to plan their own destiny. However, having seen some of the Russian troops "at play", I suggested that it would be wise if they evacuated themselves to the west.'

'That's it Colonel,' concluded Bill. 'I guess that the memory of this morning will haunt me for ever. I have taken it upon myself to send up 20 Red Cross parcels and 30 loaves of bread. I hope that is all right?'

'Well done Bill, perhaps you should follow this up tomorrow and see if there is anything further that we can do to help.'

Apart from the various objectives to secure our future, the Internal Field Force extended their patrols right round the peninsula on which *Stalag Luft* 1 was located. They came upon the bodies of two families who had decided that death was preferential to being captured by the Russians. In all, three women and two children had been shot in the head. Having searched for identity papers, they were duly buried and the graves marked by a painted headpiece. Prayers were said by the Camp Padre, the Rev. Captain Mitchell.

Victory Day

Listening to the BBC broadcasts, we realised that the Germans had been soundly beaten and that it would only be a couple of days before the transport planes would land and pull us out. Then, on Tuesday 8 May, came the wonderful news for which we had waited. Dönitz instructed all German forces to surrender and VE-Day was declared. The whole camp went wild and throughout the day and far into the night, the 'kriegies' celebrated. The Headquarters Mess of the Field Force laid on a formal dinner of which the menu was:

Tuna à la sauce tomate

. . .

Gigot d'agneau à la sauce victoire

Haricot à la mode de Boston

Purée de pommes de terre

. . .

Riz conde

. . .

Toast garnis de pâté de foie

. . .

Vin de pays   Liqueurs

. . .

Café   Bonbons

Toasts were proposed to the King and the President of the United States, The Right Honourable Winston Churchill and Marshal Stalin, our families at home, our absent friends and finally, ourselves. All very prim and proper, but I must confess that as a 'past' prisoner-of-war, it put a final seal on my seven-and-a-half months period of confinement.

The following day, somewhat chastened by a real 'humdinger' of a hangover, I and a group of officers, attended the first Free German Meeting to be held in Barth, at which a crowd of several thousand filled the main square. In our party was the camp Public Relations Officer, who subsequently issued the following report to all personnel.

HEADQUARTERS, WING X, USAAF BARTH, GERMANY

19th MAY, 1945

SUBJECT: Wing Public Relations Officers' Report on the first Free German Meeting held in Barth, 9th May, 1945.

To: All personnel.

The city of Barth turned out today to celebrate peace. A crowd of several thousand filled the square to hear addresses by the new *Burgomeister* of Barth, by the Russian Commander, and by several of the town's leading citizens. On the platform sat former *Luftwaffe* Major von Muller, one time German Intelligence Officer of *Stalag Luft* 1. The greatest part of the crowd consisted of German refugees from Pomerania, who had fled before the advancing Russian armies. They felt relief at the news that the order to cease firing had finally been issued.

The new *Burgomeister, Herr* Lemke, delivered an appeal to the people to co-operate with the new administration, to return to their old jobs and to resume their ordinary existence again. He said that the disgrace of Nazism must be removed from the German people, and that a new free nation will arise if everyone does his duty. He concluded with a promise that all German workers who had been herded into Labour Detachments in various parts of Europe would be returned to their homes and families.

The speech of the Russian Commander was translated into German by *Herr* Dahlfeld. He said: 'The Russians were not prepared for war in 1941, but the Fascists were ready. They violated the principle enunciated by Bismark, that Germany should never attack Russia. In June 1941, the German Army attacked Russia, hoping to destroy the Red Army in two months. The entire population of Russia arose to defend the homeland, and finally stopped the Germans at Stalingrad.

'We know that German propaganda reported that the Russian Army was destroyed. It was never destroyed! During the past two years, the Russians created new weapons and new forces for the final battle against Fascism. German propaganda said that the Russians want to destroy the German people. That is not true. Stalin has promised that only the militarians who brought on this war will be dealt with.

'The German people, as a people and as a Nation, shall live on, but Nazism shall die. (Cheers) Each people has its right to live on the face of the globe. Today, we are celebrating the establishment of peace with the new German Government. The war is now over. There shall be no more destruction of human life. Germany may now, in its own land, enforce order as its own people wish. They may have the political parties that they wish. Germany will rise again as a free country, as a free people working towards its future development. Today is our holiday, on which occasion I take the opportunity to wish you the best of luck for the future.'

A blind old man mounted the platform next, a refugee from Eastern Pomerania. He expressed thanks to the City administration for the fine work that they were doing. He called upon the public to adhere to the rules established by the Russian garrison. 'Now,' he concluded, 'the German people will be allowed to live as people and as human beings.'

A Barth 'Carpenter-*Meister*' read the new orders of the Russian garrison:

No weapons or cold weapons will be allowed to the people.

No-one shall be allowed outdoors between the hours of 2300 and 0500 hours.

No Russian, American, or English soldier or officer shall be billeted in any German home without an official order of the local Russian Commandant.

He stated that it was the duty of each one to see that the young women were kept indoors during the evening hours. He went on to point out that German girls had been calling to soldiers from second-storey windows, asking for cigarettes and chocolate, inviting them into their homes and then complaining of the consequences.

Speaking of the disgrace which has come upon their City with the discovery of the Concentration Camp in their vicinity and the exposé of the frightful conditions there, he said that they now knew the names of the officials responsible for the camp – they would be hunted down, and forced to clean up the filth that they had created, and to labour for the rehabilitation of the lives that they had shattered.

Referring to the destruction visited upon Germany by the Nazi regime, he pointed out that when Major von Muller had rushed out with the white flag to surrender the City of Barth, several young SS men, in disobedience of the order of their superior officer, attempted to arouse the people of the town to offer resistance to the Russians.

'You know what that would have meant? Hitler and Göbbels would have been the death of us all had they continued in power a little longer.'

He spoke of the death of the 'great American President Roosevelt' whose obituary was treated so shamefully by the German press and radio. 'That is another disgrace that the Nazis have brought upon us!'

His final words were that now that the country was at peace, there will be no more bombing and no more air-raid alarms. He too exhorted the people to return to their civilian occupations, to speed up the rebuilding of the country, and to work, each one of them, not for war and destruction, but for the production of essentials necessary for human existence.

Signed
E.D. McKenna
2nd Lt, US Air Corps
Public Relations Officer

Sixteen

Russian Trouble

Political Control

On 10 May, the platoons at the aerodrome reported that all the runways had been cleared and that they were ready to accept British and American aircraft. This news was immediately transmitted to MI6 who replied that there were priorities to clear the men in hospital first, but that we should plan to evacuate *Stalag Luft* 1 during the following week. Thrilled with the promise of an early return to England, we promptly advised Col Zchervynick, the Area Commandant. He was equally happy with the prospect of getting a large number of very impatient prisoners off his hands. We lived for the wonderful day next week when we would be whisked from our barbed-wire enclosure to return to our loved ones. Sadly that was not to be, for two days later calamity struck.

Having received a message to attend a 'Management Meeting', I made my way to Col Goodyear's office and directly I stepped inside the door, I sensed an atmosphere of tremendous tension. Sitting at the desk, looking flushed and with daggers drawn was our CO and opposite him, obviously embarrassed and expressing concern at the situation was our friend Col Z. However, it was the third senior officer who attracted my attention, mainly because he seemed to be so out of keeping with the other Russians in the room. He could well have passed as a fat little pasty-faced clerk but for a light green uniform which carried the rank of a Colonel. He had already established himself at the head of the table and slouched in his chair, puffing away at a thin cigar whilst his piggy eyes surveyed his surroundings with contempt. Then arrogantly stamping out his cigar on the carpet, he got to his feet, smoothed out his uniform and with a high pitched voice addressed Col Goodyear through Pieter, the Brigade Intelligence Officer.

'Colonel, can I presume that you have now called all the people that you require and will shortly be ready to receive my orders? Unlike you, some of us have work to do! Before I start, let us get one thing quite clear. Peace was declared four days ago and in times of peace it is the politicians who give the orders, not the military. I am the Senior

Political Officer attached to Brigade Headquarters and in all matters of major policy, I am to be consulted, not Colonel Zchervynick. Do you understand?' To emphasise this, he picked up his swagger stick and violently hit the desk.

'Now, I understand that you have announced to all and sundry that you will be evacuated from Barth aerodrome in a few days time. With whose approval may I ask?' He banged the desk once more.

'Answer me, who has given you permission?' Before our CO could reply, he shouted, 'I can tell you. No-one! You just assume that because the war is over, you can strut around giving orders. Well you can't, Colonel Goodyear. I am the person who gives orders which are . . .' He fumbled in his pocket and brought out a piece of paper from which he read.

'By virtue of the fact that the City of Barth and the surrounding areas are now Russian territory, no-one will be permitted to enter or leave without written authority from me, the Senior Political Officer.' He then hit the desk once more, turned on his heel and stalked out.

The other Russian officers with whom we had been so friendly, rather shamefacedly rose with expressive shrugs of the shoulders and turned as if to follow, but were halted in their tracks when Col Goodyear slammed his fist on the desk and shouted.

'I am damned if I will accept this instruction! Before you go will you please give me the rank, name and unit of that upstart, together with his position in your Brigade and to whom he reports. You can also tell your General that whilst the Russian Army have to take orders from politicians, I don't!'

For a moment which seemed to last an age, there was complete silence and then Col Z looking up from his feet, extended his hand in friendship. He said: 'I suggest that you report the situation to your Headquarters and let them sort out the issue at diplomatic level, because there is nothing that we can do here. Now the details that you require are . . .' He then reeled off the information.

The Russians had hardly left the room before our CO was rattling out orders. He then jumped into the jeep and, with the Radio Officer, stormed off to the aerodrome control tower. There they contacted the highest authority in MI6, explaining our situation and supplying details of the Political Officer's attitude, and were promised that the problem would receive immediate attention.

Needless to say, the buoyant and carefree attitude that had prevailed over the last few days was completely shattered and replaced by a gloomy feeling of depression. For the next 48 hours, any attempts to obtain news from our contacts at Brigade Headquarters were fobbed off with the excuse that the senior officers were at a meeting. Even Col Z failed to return our calls.

When the UK called back, they assured us that the matter was deli-
cately poised as the Russians were getting difficult about the allocation
of areas in Berlin and were using the repatriation of prisoners as a
bargaining point. Accordingly, they stressed that it was important that
we should not step out of line nor try to precipitate matters, but be
patient. With all the airmen feeling that they were on the brink of
release, this was easier said than done and there were numerous
requests from the 'kriegies' to be permitted to 'break camp'. Indeed,
Col McNeill was prompted to issue a letter to all the Field Force and I
quote from his final paragraphs:

> 'We are men – not children. We can face facts. Some of you have been
> waiting several years. A few more days will make little difference. Let us
> face this difficult and trying period patiently and cheerfully. Let us keep
> ourselves healthily occupied and make ourselves comfortable. Then,
> when we do get back, we shall be normal, healthy men and not nervous
> wrecks.'

On the following Monday morning, worse was to follow. The Political
Officer turned up at the camp and demanded to see Col Goodyear
with the Management team. From the smug attitude he adopted
when entering his quarters, we could see that we were in for further
restrictions.

'We have arrived at a solution,' he announced with a smirk. 'It is
clearly established that this is now Russian territory and, in keeping
with international practice, all your men will now require Russian passports! They will always carry them on their person as proof of identity,
and ultimately, when they wish to leave the area, they will surrender
the document to my office.'

'But,' interrupted the Colonel, 'how the hell do we secure passports
for all our men?'

Once again the beady eyes gleamed in self-satisfaction. 'Surely,
Colonel, in war you learn to adapt. Well in peace I have! I have
prepared a card, written in Russian which will be stamped officially
and issued to every member of your camp.' He then stepped forward
and with a flourish, handed the 'passport' to our astonished Colonel
who stared aghast at it.

'And when will you issue these?' Goodyear asked.

'I won't' came the curt reply. 'I am far too busy. You will make out
one of these temporary passports in the name of each person and
submit them to me for stamping.'

'But, we can't write Russian,' spluttered the Colonel.

'Then you must learn.' With that, he turned, got in his car and
drove off.

For a full minute the air was blue with blasphemy with everybody letting off steam as the impossible aspect of issuing 4600 passports in Russian sank home. Finally when we quietened down, Goodyear summed up.

'As I see it, "our friend" has now realised that he cannot stop us leaving, but he is deliberately delaying our departure and, by so doing, has saved face. Jees, what a shit! The bastard thinks that he has got us over a barrel and we will now try to negotiate. Well, we will beat him at his own game and bloody well prepare our passports . . . and in any bloody language they want!'

Preparation of Russian Passports

Turning to one of his senior officers, Goodyear said, 'Jim, this is right up your street. I am putting you in command of Operation *Passport*. I will give you this morning to size up the problem and I suggest that it might be wise to inspan a couple of chaps to help your thinking, but let's get cracking as soon as possible.'

Thus started a major project, which to the credit of Jim and his buddies, was planned to the smallest degree. The immediate problem was to find the draughtsmen and a broadcast was made over the loud-speaker system advising the 'kriegies' of the latest Russian edict and calling for volunteers. We finally rustled up about 50 chaps, who, under the tuition of our Russian-speaking officer, Hank, painstakingly became indoctrinated in copying the characters on the sample. When interpreted it read:

RUSSIAN PASSPORT

This passport is issued to . . . . who will be subject to the laws and regulations of the Occupying Power.

STAMP

With some of the team cutting cards down to size and drawing lines, the balance split into two shifts, each with an 'inspector' and commenced the slow and tedious task of copying the Russian characters. Once the draughtsmen got the hang of the letters, it became a routine slog but, as we were determined that no 'kriegie' would be turned back due to a faulty document, our inspection was particularly strict. Even so, it took about 10 minutes to prepare a card and, with the heavy concentration required, we could only work for an hour at a time and then had to have a break. We worked in shifts, solidly day and night, over the next 36 hours and finally licked the job late on Wednesday. An administrative team had inserted the names and these were checked and double checked so that 'passports' were ready for stamping just three days after the bombshell.

The speed at which we overcame the hurdle to our evacuation completely astounded the Political Officer whose only comment was 'It seems as if you really want to leave us.' Fortunately, the Soviet Brigade Commander was sympathetic and immediately inspanned the complete Orderly Room staff for stamping and within five hours all the cards were handed back to us. Before leaving, I asked Pieter to obtain a written clearance from the Commander and the Political Officer stating that subject to the surrender of the 'passports', we had completed the necessary emigration requirements. Armed with this valuable document, we joyfully returned to our camp.

Flight to Freedom

It was then a case of contacting MI6 who called back to give us the welcome news that squadrons of Super Fortresses would be arriving the following day, and that their Operational teams would be contacting us to tie up details. With the sudden realisation that we might – subject to the whims of the Political Officer – be back in the UK by the next evening, we all got down to packing our treasures in our Red Cross parcel boxes, which was the limitation placed on our baggage. I had only a few personal things like my diary and odd documents that I had collected, and was therefore able to provide space for some of the chaps in my room who, over the years, had assembled other items.

The actual planning of the evacuation was in the hands of Camp Management who prepared the order of embarkation in which the names of the passengers were pre-listed. Apart from those who were unable to march to the aerodrome and for whom special transport was organised, the 'kriegies' were to be marshalled into plane loads before leaving the camp. As a matter of pride, the senior Allied Officers ordered that the barracks were to be left clean and tidy and that items such as blankets were to be handed into the main store. Col Z then suggested that one of his staff, accompanied by the Mayor of Barth, should officially take the barracks over together with the sporting and educational equipment and organise distribution amongst the refugees.

Whether the Russians commandeered any of the items, we don't know, but at least we left our 'enforced home' in good order, having first ensured that food and Red Cross parcels, in excess of our own requirements, were given to the doctor at the French Concentration Camp.

At last all was ready and when the big day dawned, I prayed that everything would work out smoothly. As Adjutant my job was to act as liaison with the Russians and I had organised a number of guides to lead each plane load past the 'Emigration Officials' to surrender their passports before entering the aircraft. I had placed myself at the end of the table occupied by the Political Officer and his staff. With the assistance of Hank, our interpreter, pure hot coffee and schnapps, we were soon working in harmony.

I suppose that we had been waiting patiently on the side of the tarmac for an hour when, away in the distance, we could discern wave upon wave of bombers flying towards us. As they came nearer, so the roar of their powerful engines increased and many of the 'old timers' just broke down and cried, whilst others could be seen offering up a prayer of thankfulness for their survival. Soon we could see them quite clearly as they lined up to approach the runway. Lowering their wheels, they applied flaps and with perfect precision, landed, one after the other to the wild cheers of those waiting. It was like the operation of a full squadron returning after a raid, as the leading aircraft cleared the end of the runway to taxi slowly round the perimeter track.

At the lead-in tarmac to the main runway, where the aircraft halted, we checked away every load with our new-made friends. Within seconds, the waiting 'kriegies' were up and in the bomber, the hatch closed and the huge plane would move forward to prepare for take-off. The Americans had brought their own ground crew of 'Air Controllers' who dispatched the aircraft, one every two minutes. Hardly had the first squadron departed, when there on the horizon, were the next bunch.

The backchat between the carefree aircrew and the overwhelmingly joyful PoWs really made our job a happy one and time seemed to pass quickly. Indeed, I suddenly realised that most of the chaps had gone and that the Field Force were beginning to line up. So, please God, it would soon be the rear party and that meant Col McNeill and myself.

I had arranged to keep back six Red Cross parcels in case of an emergency and these I then gave as a farewell gift to the 'passport collectors'. They were absolutely delighted and followed us all the way to our waiting aircraft and then, what do you know, the Political Officer got up and came towards us to shake hands. Taking a piece of paper from his pocket he proudly read:

'Goodbye and good luck. Perhaps we shall meet again.'

'Not on your Nelly,' I replied with a grin and with a final wave climbed into the body of the Fortress.

What a wonderful moment it was to see one of the crew lock the door clamps and to give the thumbs-up sign to the pilot. Then came the revving up of the engines, the surge forward and finally the lift off into the heavens and freedom. Perhaps at last, I could say, 'For me the war is over'.

INDEX